RESPONSIBILITY CENTER MANAGEMENT

A Guide to Balancing
Academic Entrepreneurship with
Fiscal Responsibility

JOHN R. CURRY
ANDREW L. LAWS
JON C. STRAUSS

Library of Congress Cataloging-in-Publication Data

Curry, John R.
  Responsibility center management : a guide to balancing academic
entrepreneurship with fiscal responsibility / by John R. Curry, Andrew L.
Laws, Jon C. Strauss.
      pages cm
  Includes bibliographical references and index.
  ISBN 978-1-56972-012-7
  1. Universities and colleges--Business management. 2. Universities and
colleges--Administration. 3. Universities and colleges--Finance. I. Title.
  LB2341.92.C87 2013
  378.1'06--dc23

                                          2013003588

Editorial Management: Tadu Yimam, Director, Online Learning, NACUBO
Design and Layout: Zaki Ghul, Consultant

NC4070

CONTENTS

ACKNOWLEDGMENTS

The authors have benefitted over many years from literally hundreds of conversations with colleagues and friends about financial management in general and incentive-based approaches in particular. In addition to thanking again those individuals who made our first edition possible, we would like to acknowledge new contributors who helped us develop the current edition by providing insights into their own universities, adding to the intellectual foundations of Responsibility Center Management, offering grist for our case studies, and in some cases providing vigorous critiques of early drafts:

Paul N. Courant
University of Michigan Librarian and Dean of Libraries (and former Provost)
University of Michigan

Barbara A. Feiner
Vice Chancellor for Finance
Washington University in St. Louis

Bonnie C. Gibson
Vice President, Budget and Management Analysis
University of Pennsylvania

John R Gilliom,
Professor of Political Science and Associate Dean,
College of Arts and Sciences, Ohio University

Stephen T. Golding,
Vice President for Finance and Administration,
Ohio University

Larry Goldstein,
President,
Campus Strategies LLC

Aimee S. Heeter,
Associate Vice Provost and Director of Budget,
Planning and Development
Indiana University, Bloomington

Lisa Montgomery
Vice President for Finance and Administration
Medical University of South Carolina

Martha E. Pollack
Provost and Executive Vice President for Academic Affairs
University of Michigan

Douglas Priest
Associate Vice Chancellor for Budgetary Administration
University of Indiana, Bloomington

Amir Rahnamay-Azar,
Vice President for Finance and Chief Financial Officer,
Carnegie Mellon University

Mark S. Sothmann,
Vice President for Academic Affairs and Provost,
Medical University of South Carolina

Brett Sweet
Vice Chancellor for Finance and Chief Financial Officer
Vanderbilt University

Timothy S. Tracy,
Dean of College of Pharmacy,
University of Kentucky

Jeffrey S. Vitter,
Provost & Executive Vice Chancellor,
University of Kansas

Charles E. Young
Chancellor Emeritus
University of California, Los Angeles

John Wilton,
Vice Chancellor for Administration & Finance,
University of California, Berkeley

We would also like to thank **Megan Cluver** of the Huron Consulting Group
for her considerable help with the Bibliography.

PREFACE
The Rationale for a New Edition

Changing economic fortunes in the last decade have led universities to intensify focus on incentives for revenue growth and financial accountability, the foundations of responsibility center management (RCM).

When we wrote the first edition of this book in 2002, only a handful of universities operated under RCM. Seasoned players included Harvard, the University of Pennsylvania, and the University of Southern California; recent entries included Indiana University and the University of Michigan. The private universities' motivations were to aid and abet revenue growth to enhance their competitive positions. Among public universities, the driving forces were declining state support and the need to engage more hunter-gatherers in foraging for revenues to supplant losses.

Such forces ebb and flow over time and are back at work today with a vengeance, especially so in public universities because of the burgeoning structural budget deficits within their states. Public universities now more than ever are recognizing that they have to rethink their business models given the shrinking share of discretionary state revenues. RCM is one such model. As best we can count, less than a dozen universities operated under RCM in 2002. Today 14.2% of universities self-report having an RCM model and, not surprising given the times, interest among public universities in RCM is soaring, with more than 21% of public doctoral institutions reporting that they use an RCM model according to the *2011 Inside Higher Education Survey of College and University Business Officers.*

Moreover, earlier adopters of formal decentralized management structures continue to refine their approaches. Some RCM universities have moved toward greater centralization, the University of Southern California and Vanderbilt being among them. Indiana University has created a larger pool of central resources to fund university-wide initiatives. And the University of Michigan has revised its thinking from the original RCM design through two iterations, with its recent approaches to cost allocation and filling the reallocation pool being of special interest. Given all this activity, the literature on RCM—or, more broadly, incentive-based budgeting—has grown enormously. In addition to new and strong anecdotal testimony, several behavioral studies have emerged that are worth our attention. We have a much larger palette and a much richer history to report and evaluate than we did in 2002.

For readers who may not be familiar with RCM, let's reprise the essential features:

- Tuition and research revenues are allocated to the colleges and schools (responsibility centers) that generate them;
- Facilities and central administration costs are allocated to responsibility centers in proportion to space occupied and central services consumed;
- A central pool of resources (often called the subvention pool), assembled through either direct central ownership of specific revenues or taxes applied to school revenues or direct expenses, is allocated to compensate for disciplinary unit-cost/price imbalances and to support university priorities.

Together, these funds flows distribute and connect authority and responsibility further down the organization chart and create a number of potentially powerful incentives:

- Centers are responsible for meeting revenue projections and living within their planned operating margins;
- Incentives for growth include retention of new revenues;
- Incentives for prudent management include retention of operating surpluses and repayment of operating deficits; and
- Incentives to optimize space usage and to limit central overhead costs reside in the abilities of the centers to spend dollars saved in reduced space usage and administrative costs allocated to them.

RCM structures have developed over time for reasons well beyond the desire or need for additional revenues. Perhaps the biggest reason is a fundamental decoupling of academic authority from financial responsibility. While decentralization of authority in universities is a natural act, decentralization of responsibility is not.

Examples of decoupling of academic authority from financial responsibility abound in universities. Faculty members make decisions within departments about curriculum, admissions requirements, class size, and numbers of sections offered. Such decisions can have major impacts on enrollments and hence tuition revenues, and are all too often uninformed by their financial consequences. Revenues are someone else's problem: the provost's, the admissions director's, or the chief financial officer's. Faculty members may apply for and win a research award with implications for additional laboratory space, which has financial consequences for central administrators responsible for space allocation, renovation, and construction. But that's someone else's problem, too! Responsibility Center Management attempts to couple such academic decisions with their financial consequences by making a fundamental trade: ownership of revenues for financial responsibility, including the full costs of programs.

While critics often suggest that RCM replaces a university's academic focus with a financial one, they forget that academic expectations and standards can and should be imbedded in any budget development process. RCM's alignment of financial accountability with revenue ownership simply highlights an institution's internal economy better to enable entrepreneurship and enhance both local and central decision-making.

Having been part of the history and evolution of RCM, either as chief budget and financial officers or consultants, since its origins at the University of Pennsylvania through its current implementations at a number of new adopters, we want to reprise what we have learned now some 11 years beyond our evaluation of the first 25 years in our first edition. In this new edition, we will:

- Place RCM in the context of external and internal forces leading to new and evolving budget and financial management models—to address the question, RCM as opposed to what? (Chapter 1).

- Address the managerial foundations for RCM, especially the benefits of coupling academic authority with financial responsibility—and the pathologies that can emerge from decoupling (Chapter 2).

- Provide primers—both short and long versions—for designing RCM systems (Chapter 3).

- Address how RCM is working from the perspectives of early and recent writings on the subject: what the literature has to say (Chapter 4).

- Provide our own assessment of how RCM is working based on academic studies, internal university reports, new interviews, case studies and observations since 2002: to contrast promise with performance (Chapters 5 and 6).

- Give examples of how RCM provides a ready foundation for new kinds of management analyses (Chapter 7).

- Recommend a multi-step approach to implementing RCM along with characteristics of successful implementations (Chapter 8).

- Address leadership roles of financial officers in RCM (Chapter 9).

- Provide a very brief summation (Chapter 10).

- Include appendices that list the institutions that employ RCM-like models and provide answers to frequently asked questions about RCM compiled from our own leadership, management, and consulting roles.

As a point of clarity, we note that throughout this book the term RCM will subsume the variety of revenue-based incentive systems operating at the many universities we discuss. Indeed, the term RCM actually evolved within its originating university! When conceived at the University of Pennsylvania, this model was initially called "Responsibility Center Budgeting." It was soon understood, however, that the model is more than just formats and rules to organize budget development: the model is a potentially powerful management tool. The initial name was thus revised in favor of "Responsibility Center *Management.*" This term was altered again during design and implementation at the University of Southern California: When it was noted that the essence of the model is the focus on revenues, RCM became "*Revenue* Center Management." Over the ensuing years, still other naming conventions have evolved. Herein, we will attempt to refer to specific institutional models with their adopted names, though the authors will use RCM generically to refer to the principled model.

And *so,* as we did in 2002, we have a simple goal in this new edition: to answer the question, "How is responsibility center management working?" Is it the work of deities or the work of the devil? It continues to amaze us 11 years hence just how many fundamental and strategic academic and financial questions can be extracted from an RCM model when the numbers begin to change and ownership of the increments is at stake.

A final note and caveat: Like its predecessor, this new edition is not intended to be a scholarly work. We have not reviewed all the literature nor have we dissected and assessed all instances of RCM. Our surveys and interviews have not been structured to yield comparative quantitative results. Thus, our conclusions will be more experientially based and personally reasoned than purely data driven.

Although we have been involved with the development of decentralized and incentive-based approaches to budgeting and financial management for almost 40 years, we may not have properly credited or interpreted all the work of others. Please let us know about any misinterpretations or otherwise further enlighten us by sharing your own experiences about how RCM is working.

John R. Curry
Andrew L. Laws
Jon C. Strauss
June 2013

CHAPTER ONE

RCM: A Response to Changing Times and Complex Environments

RCM was developed and has evolved over some 35 years in response to multiple forces: changes in the external environment—the larger economic context; needs within universities to achieve a balance between academic authority and financial responsibility; desires to unleash and provide structure to entrepreneurship; the need to have realistic measures of the quality, cost, and growth of administrative services; and the increasing imperative to understand the full costs attending academic programs. In this chapter, we focus on the evolution of budgeting in general and RCM's place in it by describing three of the most common approaches to budgeting along with their attendant strengths and weaknesses.

Driving the evolution of both budgeting practices and the attendant literature are the changing economic and political contexts of recent decades. Indeed, ad hoc responses to external stimuli and growing environmental complexity have given rise to organizational adaptations, which in turn have inspired (sometimes) thoughtful rationalizations and new approaches to budgeting.

While there have been many economic and political forces in play, we note the following as relevant here:

- The advent of federally sponsored research in the aftermath of World War II, which began devolution of authority to faculty members in proportion to the grant dollars they secured, changing the balance between teaching and research, and diversifying university revenue portfolios—and ownership of resources;

- Changes in the federal government's Office of Management and Budget rules to allow for the recovery of research-related administrative and facilities costs;

- The emergence and proliferation of a complex variety of professional degree, certificate, and outreach programs; the recognition of the different enrollment markets governing each; and the acknowledgement of increased competition within those markets;

- The Bayh-Dole Act, which enabled universities to own the intellectual capital derived from faculty research sponsored by the federal government—and the devolution of that ownership and the resources flowing there from to departments and individuals involved;

- The "crowding out" of discretionary components of state budgets by entitlement programs, law enforcement, and K-12 demands with consequent reductions in state support of public universities, and the emerging of privatization activities in response; and, *a fortiori,*

- The shifting cost-burden of education: In 1987, state appropriations represented 76.7% of educational revenue per student, whereas 25 years later, in 2012, state appropriations represented only 53.2% of educational revenue per student—and in many states much less (Lingenfelter, 2012).

New markets and market stratification bring added economic complexity and the potential for diversified revenue growth. Successfully adaptive organizations become complex in proportion to the environments they confront. Accordingly, universities have become more complex. Market stratification has given rise to market specialists and decentralization of focus and management within universities. Decentralized focus and management lead to claims of ownership of revenues generated.

New markets have brought new stakeholders—new "owners"—and their influence on institutional direction and demands for accountability have increased: from federal funding agencies, to corporate underwriters, to bond holders and rating agencies, to donors, and alumni. The reduction in state support for public universities has created new sensitivities to markets beyond one's legislature and state boundaries and is challenging the very nature of public higher education. (See Duderstadt in Burke, et al (2007) for further elucidation of the forces driving decentralization in universities.)

In response, universities are changing the ways they fund and finance education and research. In most cases, responses have been program-specific, incentive-based but ad hoc, ranging from:

• Revenue sharing deals for certain streams of tuition and research dollars;

• Sharing and carry-forward of operating surpluses;

• The creation of special centers to be funded from uniquely attributable revenues; and

• Sharing of patent license revenues with faculty "inventors" and the departments and service units that support their work.

While such responses have created avenues for entrepreneurship and led to revenue enhancements, they have mostly developed organically, with limited methodical analysis and tremendous political influence. The end result for many universities is a smattering of complex and inconsistent policies. A confirming anecdote: We recently were told by the chief financial officer of a large public university, "We have so many handshake agreements and hallway deals for revenue sharing that I cannot identify them."

RCM models have been implemented at many universities in an attempt to extract coherence from their emerging "adhocracies" through the application of systematic analysis, the design of consistent policies, and the unveiling of the institution's internal economy.

COMMON UNIVERSITY BUDGET MODELS

We will examine three common approaches to budgeting in higher education: (1) *incremental*, (2) *formula-based*, and (3) *revenue-centered (RCM)*[1]. Incremental budgeting is the most common: decisions are centrally driven; changes are at the margins of historical base budgets. Formula-based budget decisions are also made centrally but use policy formulas to relate inputs such as enrollment or research volume or outputs such as graduation rates to funding levels. RCM models devolve revenue ownership and allocate indirect costs to operating units. Budget decisions are shared among the centers with their revenue availability and central administration with its subvention pool.

Incremental Budgeting: This model is characterized by central ownership of all unrestricted sources. It is a top-down approach to budget development, with the view that the current budget is the "base" to which increments (salary and inflation adjustments, new faculty positions, and so on) are added to build next year's budget. The budget development process typically begins

---

1 For a more comprehensive list of approaches to budgeting in higher education, we refer you to *A Guide to College and University Budgeting, Foundations for Institutional Effectiveness* (Goldstein, 2012).

with the provost, CFO, and the central budget office projecting next year's unrestricted revenues: Tuition, indirect cost recoveries (F&A), investment income, unrestricted gift flows are the primary sources. Then they determine appropriate salary pools and inflation adjustments for non-salary expenses. The difference between projected revenues and projected expenses becomes the pool available for incremental programmatic allocations.

As these projections are being completed, the central administration issues a budget call letter to deans and administrative directors, typically describing the decision parameters governing top and bottom line budget projections, the resulting availability of new resources—or reduction in current resources—to address new needs and initiatives, and the priorities (sometimes derived from a strategic plan) that will govern budget decisions. Deans and directors then prepare budget (expense) letters itemizing line-item requests and send them to the provost and/or the CFO. Budget hearings, ranging from relatively private conversations in the provost's office to presentations to institutional budget advisory committees then ensue, followed by evaluations of requests from whatever groups are involved in the hearings, and final decisions made by the provost and/or CFO and the president.

When projected revenues are less than projected expenses in this incremental universe, the budget call letter will typically impose across-the-board reduction targets (X%), and will ask that letters from deans and directors describe actions they will take, and their consequences to programs, to meet their reduction targets.

Strengths and Weaknesses

These centralized incremental models have had remarkable staying power, and they characterize the modal budgeting approach among colleges and universities today. Indeed, they were totally appropriate when the dominant sources of revenues were state appropriations and undergraduate tuition revenues in better days. To some, this model is a financial reification of the "one university" ideal: We are all in this together, deriving sustenance from a common source and participating on an equal footing, with shares of the common pie differing minimally among us over time. When base allocations are appropriately managed, the model putatively puts a very large steering wheel in the hands of senior leadership: the sum of all unrestricted revenues. The ability to steer the university toward central priorities is apparently maximized, and funding of multidisciplinary activities is relatively simple.

The model is also simple to administer. Indeed, during budget development, deans and directors make cases only for increases in expense budgets. And during the play out of actuals within the period governed by the budget, it is relatively simple to manage from the individual unit business officer's perspective. Since one manages only expenses, most of which are salaries and benefits, if one encumbers these at, say a quarterly review of budget performance, then salary savings or potential overruns are clear; only the non-salary components and future personnel appointments need be monitored. Demands on financial management skills are relatively low.

But appearances differ from reality. Central incremental budget decisions over time typically maintain a school's relative share of the total expense pie, but just as typically will *not* lead to shares in proportion to teaching and research support demands as reflected by changes in credit hours taught or sponsored dollars delivered by the school's faculty. While theoretically, such a mal-distribution relative to demand can be addressed in a centralized model, the time lag in addressing the problem is long given the organizational distance of the decider from the impact, and the fact that the only marginal resources for addressing the problem are likely to be part of another school's base budget. Related is the fact that base budgets become "entitlements" over a very short period: Even though their source appears to be centrally "owned," the schools have laid claims. As with real estate, occupancy is 90% of the law! Central steering is diminished accordingly. Thus can a sense of inappropriate entitlements emerge to challenge the legitimacy of the centralized budgeting model along with its putative companion, the one-university concept.

This model also puts an enormous burden on central officers, typically the provost and CFO. From a budgeting standpoint, conversations mostly go one way: from dean or director to senior officer asking for money. And as Cook and Dunworth (2007) observe, there is no downside to requesting more budget than you need when it's someone else's money and next year's increment is a function of what you already have.

Finally, centralized budget models typically do not adequately engage (if they do so at all) the full range of resource growth happening all around. For example, through the individual entrepreneurship of the faculty, sponsored research may be growing in several schools, but the effects on central and local services and on capital requirements are typically not the purview of the formal budget process. At the same time, new markets for educational services may be recognized in schools and departments, but the potential revenues for these may go untapped for want of explicit and known gain-sharing incentives. The combination can lead to suboptimal resource development and deployment.

Formula-Based Budgeting: Formula-based budget models have evolved to address the kinds of imbalances between demands and resources available that arise when budgets are developed incrementally. Decisions are still made centrally, but based on policies that relate inputs such as enrollment or research volume to determine funding levels. Here, budgets ebb and flow with demand.

Performance-based formulas may reward consequences, such as increased retention and graduation rates or reductions in time to degree.

According to the *2011 Inside Higher Ed College Business Officer Survey*, 26% of institutions use demand-based formula funding models and 20% use performance-based models. Resources flow to academic units in one of two ways. In the most common approach, funds (say, tuition revenue) are pooled and allocations made to reflect proportional unit shares (the formula). For example, a college teaching 10% of the credit hours would receive 10% of the tuition pool. Such a formula distributes the pool toward the unit generating the largest share of credit hours. A constant or shrinking pie is redistributed, but incentives exist to grow one's own share. On the other hand, performance formulas, rewarding say increasing graduation rates or recruiting more people in the top 20% of the high-school class, distribute the pool based on outcomes not teaching demand.

Formula funding models are sometimes modified to incorporate weighting schemes. The most common is a credit-hour weighting to account for differential delivery costs of instruction. The average weight across disciplines and professions in a university might be normalized at 1, for example. The college of engineering might be awarded a weight of 1.8, indicating that each of its credit hours is 1.8 times as expensive to deliver as the average. If engineering's share of the credit hour pool is 10%, its weighted share becomes 18%. Thus are weighting formulas combined with tuition apportionment formulas discussed in the earlier paragraph.

Another common modification involves the portion of resources to which metrics apply. Not all university activities—central administration, for example—easily lend themselves to funding via formulas. Thus, the portion of the total unrestricted pool needed to pay for administrative services reduces the pool available for formula funding of academic units. Similarly, not all academic activities—research and public service for example—easily tie to units of input or output. Consequently, formula funding models are often confined to small margins of overall activities. The University of Tennessee, for instance, has incorporated performance funding into its resource management model although almost 95% of funds continue to be allocated as base budgets. That leaves only 5% to flow at the margin. Reducing the portion of resources flowing through the formula can significantly weaken incentives and impede reallocations needed to meet demand, and when taken too far, can eviscerate incentives and the sense of fairness entirely.

Strengths and Weaknesses

Both formula-based models provide an objective method for making budget decisions, and they are easy to understand. Metrics enable measuring and rewarding success. Input formulas can promote internal funding equity and redistribute resources from shrinking to growing programs—if applied symmetrically. Performance-based formulas can promote mission. By combining both kinds of metrics, institutions can work toward optimizing their respective models.

Like all good things, however, these models have their limitations. First, the development of formula-based models can be difficult given that simple formulas may be too simple, program unit costs are not always easy to ascertain, and academic quality considerations (not to mention politics) mediate most any metric design. Second, since central administrators apply the metrics, they may be unwilling to confront the politics of budget reallocation implied by the metrics: The upside is easy, and the downside fraught with the same issues as reducing a base budget in a non-metric-based system, with the central administration being the bearer of the bad news that the formulas require taking budget back.

We should also note in closing this section that the formulas we have seen most often have been developed by states to make sense of their allocations to their public universities. These universities in turn may or may not use the same formulas to allocate the money to departments and schools.

Revenue-Centered Budgeting: Revenue-centered budgeting *(RCM in more descriptive terms to emphasize what distinguishes this model from the prior two)* provides incentives for all entrepreneurial activities with particular focus on *all* revenues. The approach devolves revenue ownership and allocates all indirect costs to units whose programs generate and consume them respectively. The model utilizes "subvention" to achieve balance between local optimization and investment in the best interest of the university as a whole.

RCM attempts to address the weaknesses inherent in the approaches discussed above. Specifically:

- Enrollment and research markets, and the schools, departments, and individuals engaging those markets most directly, are recognized by formally sharing set portions of tuition and research-related revenues among schools and departments. Such devolution of revenue ownership is intended to aid and abet local entrepreneurship and growth in both the deans' and the university's top lines.

- Indirect costs supporting instruction and research—facilities and administration—are made explicit and allocated to the schools and auxiliaries according to space occupied and estimates of administrative services consumed.

- The difference between (1) the school's revenues and (2) the sum of direct and allocated indirect costs is funded through allocation from central administration sources (we'll call these *university revenues* or *subventions*): central shares of tuition and unrestricted research revenues, state appropriations, unrestricted investment income, or direct expense taxes, for example. This "difference" is typically a function of priorities governing annual budget development, and a recognition of differential costs of instruction across units, which typically charge common tuition per credit hour.

- In exchange for shared ownership of tuition and research-related revenues, deans and directors take responsibility (hence the "R" in RCM) for bottom-line impacts of revenue variances. If revenues exceed budget plans, they flow to the bottom line and are carried forward. Similarly, revenue shortfalls are repaid either through local expense hold-backs during the year, reductions in fund balances, or payments from future years' budgets.

The budget development process begins typically with a budget call letter from the provost and/or the CFO in much the same way as incremental budgeting. The call letter outlines the top-down estimates of university-wide revenues, with first-order estimates of key planning variables: tuition increases, salary pool requirements, non-salary inflation adjustments, and the like. Other issues like prospects for state funding or changes in benefits and utilities costs are taken into account as well. The letter goes on to describe central priorities guiding allocations of university revenues for the coming year(s), provide estimates of changes in indirect costs, and make preliminary allocations of university revenue (subvention) to each responsibility center.

At this point, the RCM approach diverges materially from centralized approaches from the responder's vantage. Deans and directors prepare budget *proposals* (as opposed to simply requests for more money) which:

- Project their shares of tuition, research, and other revenues;

- Raise issues affecting the preliminary estimates of their shares of indirect costs and propose revisions; and

- Describe how they would balance their proposed budgets if their preliminary allocations of university revenues differed from their current levels (either more or less).

In developing their proposals, deans now put their own shares of revenues into play. Once this takes place, budget meetings take on a very different character.

First, they involve a joint discussion of revenues. If, for example, the sum of the deans' projections of tuition and research revenues exceeds overall university estimates, reconciliation needs to begin. The conversation may involve the interplay of local recruitment of students and the central admissions office's estimates of incoming classes; it may involve estimates of changes in student course-taking patterns internally; or it may involve planned and expected revenue growth attending the launch of a new program. In other words, a joint understanding of external and internal student markets begins to evolve. Analogous observations can be obtained with respect to research and other revenues.

Second, a discussion of indirect costs ensues since these are now visible, consume revenues, and thus constrain resources available for direct expenses across the schools and auxiliaries. Such conversations range from the quality of the services received, to the efficiency with which they are delivered, to their redundancy with services provided within the schools, to hopes for services not currently provided, to the legitimacy of the indirect cost allocation rules. Feedback to internal service providers typically follows such conversations and may influence facilities and administrative services budgets. Outsourcing options may also be considered.

Third, a discussion of relative and joint priorities ensues. This conversation normally leads to mutual understanding: what a dean's budget proposal will accomplish with respect to school-specific strategic plans and priorities; the extent to which local (the school's) priorities are consistent with university priorities; and the university's expectations that will be imbedded in the allocation of university revenues to the school.

Fourth, allocations of university revenues across the centers are set in the context of rebalancing the whole through the vetting and refining of revenue projections and service centers' proposals, the latter affecting the costs allocated to the schools and auxiliaries.

Fifth, final budget proposals constrained by all the above are submitted and approved.

The provost's and CFO's decisions about changes in university-revenue allocations to schools can be in the context of proposed single line items that comprise an increment, or in the context of a proposed block grant derived from a high-level business plan proposed by a dean, or as limited-term underwriting of a new initiative.

A prototypical RCM budget involving two schools and administration, and exhibiting the features discussed above can be found in Table 1, Chapter 3. More elaborated versions will appear as we get into further details in the subsequent chapters.

Strengths and Weaknesses

As we noted earlier, RCM evolved in response to the weaknesses inherent in centralized models. Devolution of revenue ownership recognizes increasing market stratification and complexity, creates incentives for top-line growth, and distributes revenue authority and responsibility more broadly. Distributed ownership of revenues enhances local options to deal with local budget issues: the frequency of requests to the provost for more money decreases, allowing more time for focus on larger strategic issues. Conversations between provost and dean are now two ways: the provost can ask how the dean proposes to fund budget needs with *his* revenues as counterpoint to the typical dean's request for the provost to solve his problems with *her* revenue.

▶ INDIRECT COSTS, OVERHEAD, AND INDIRECT COST RECOVERIES (F&A)

Throughout this edition, we will use the terms "indirect costs" and "overhead" interchangeably to denote costs incurred on behalf of the primary (direct) university activities of education, research, and public service. Indirect costs comprise a university's central facilities, administration, and service costs.

Readers should differentiate these "indirect" or "overhead" *costs* from "indirect cost *recoveries*," as the latter are the revenues that institutions receive from outside sponsors to cover facilities and administration costs supporting direct sponsored activities. These revenues are often called simply, "F&A." Throughout this edition, when we are referring to these revenues, we will say "indirect cost recoveries (F&A)".

In sum, the degree of engagement in how the university works financially and the relationships among budgets, academic outputs (teaching, research, and service), program quality, and the roles of administrative support services are vastly increased. Transparency is enabled: All revenue and expense budgets are in sight, as are the gross and net operating margins of the schools and the subventions that balance them out. (Of course, university leaders must be willing to share the RCM reports.)

While RCM was designed—and continues to be designed—to address weaknesses in other approaches, it gives rise to issues of its own. At the onset of RCM design and implementation, the question arises, what are the "right" revenue allocation rules? Should tuition revenues be allocated in proportion to credit hours taught, or the students' majoring schools, or both? Since costs of educating students occur in both the teaching and the enrolling (majoring) school, the answer is "both." Since the school providing students with courses incurs the preponderance of costs, credit hours generated should be the primary driver of tuition allocations. The typical split is 80% based on credit hours and 20% based on locus of major. In most universities using versions of RCM, such tensions are minimal.

Devolution of state appropriations to local levels presents several issues. The question arises, "Should there be any formal devolution at all?" In some state university RCM systems, the state appropriation is the primary source of university revenues (or subvention) and is allocated from the center to the schools on both university-priority and cost-of-program bases. In other RCM state universities, appropriations may be viewed as tuition or research surrogates and apportioned on credit-hour or research-volume bases—or both.

Of more concern is the fact that many universities using RCM report that they have devolved too large a percentage of revenues to schools and departments, thus reducing the central ability to underwrite strategic initiatives and otherwise steer the institution. Compounding this is the fact that, just as with base expense budgets, the schools' shares of university revenues in RCM can succumb to the entitlement disease (Strauss and Curry, 2002). Annual refreshing of the rationales underlying allocation of university revenues to the schools and retention of a defined portion of the pool to underwrite new ventures (which may grow into important continuing programs, warranting a new discussion) are countervailing forces.

Another perceived but not necessarily real weakness is that, with the devolution of revenues, local optimization will come to dominate at the expense of global optimization; there will be underinvestment in the commons. The natural and potentially constructive tension between central and local perspectives and priorities, and over indirect costs that support the commons, often provides rich context for conversations about the common good. (See Cantor and Courant (2008) for more on this issue.) The key here, again, is the balance between local and centrally retained revenues.

Indirect cost allocation rules give rise to the greatest tension in RCM. They seem to provide a perfect forum for pie divider virtuosi. However, any change in rules creates winners and losers and does not increase revenues. *From least provocative to most:* Facilities allocations (janitorial services, utilities, minor repairs, sometimes depreciation) are the least contentious provided that occupancy data are accurate and current, utilities are metered to each building, and janitorial service costs and quality compare favorably with outside vendor prices. General administration, information technology, development, student services, and library costs are all almost equally contentious, a function of the legitimacy of a variety of possible allocation rules, and local desires to perform and fund their own customer-specific versions of central services.

To the extent that allocation rules become contentious—and members of academic communities are especially adroit at criticism—a form of Gresham's Law obtains: the bad currency of pie-dividing talk drives out the good currency of pie-expansion focus (Curry, in Whalen, 1991). Many RCM universities seem to have made peace with such rules over long periods of time; others have made major changes in the way they exhibit and allocate them just to quiet things down—at least temporarily.

While some might argue that the issues we have been discussing are weaknesses, they give rise to new forms of engagement that are not spawned in centralized approaches. The ensuing constructive tensions can be a benefit—as long as they remain constructive.

A FAMILY ANALOGY

A medical school dean at one of our clients provided a simple anecdote to explain how she experienced the transition from an incremental model to an RCM model. The dean noted that the institution's incremental model allocated resources much like a family with a child, explaining that when the child wants a new bicycle, he goes to his parents and pleads for the bike. The child has no real idea of the bike's full cost or his parents' annual earnings or priorities; he simply wants the bike and makes his pitch.

In contrast, the dean continued, the child in a family following an RCM model would know the rules for getting a new bike: He would be expected to generate his own resources to purchase the bike but knows he needs his parents' blessing to take on a paper route—and they just might supplement his earnings if he makes the right case!

Central models typically lack this second option because local revenue options are not explicit; they are the exception rather than the rule. Thus, the system limits incentives for distributed entrepreneurship and fails to maximize the potential for top-line growth. See Massy, for example, in Burke, et al (2007). (Author's note: By sharing this anecdote, we do not intend to demean the many quality arguments that deans make with provosts in centralized systems.)

For more details and the contextual workings of RCM see Whalen (1991); Curry in Whalen (1991); Curry, Strauss, and Whalen in Massy, (1996); Strauss and Curry (2002); Cantor and Courant (2003); Hearn, et al (2006); Duderstadt in Burke, et al (2007); Massy in Burke, et al (2007); Maddox (2007); Nelson (2007); Hanover (2008); Zeppos (2010); and Vonasek (2011). And still more in subsequent chapters of this edition.

Mixed Models: There are of course examples of formal mixtures. Green's 2011 Inside Higher Ed survey included approximately 2,350 two- and four-year colleges and universities, each which enrolls 500 or more students. A total of 606 campus and system chief business or financial officers completed the survey. One of the survey questions asked about the type of budget model their respective institutions employed. The sum of institutional selections significantly exceeds 100%, as many institutions deploy multiple models. All told, just over half of the surveyed institutions noted that their model reflected more than one described model, suggesting hybrid implementations and/or alternative implementation for operating units within a single institution.

Stanford, for one, has explicit agreements with Business and Medicine, the "formula schools," which incorporate most components of RCM; similar arrangements govern auxiliaries. The rest of Stanford operates within a centralized incremental or block-grant structure. Important to note: Stanford has almost inelastic demand for education and limits undergraduate enrollment. Thus incentives for increasing enrollment are not needed. Moreover, each school has significant endowments—locally "owned"—to underwrite a portion of its academic programs. These are more important observations than they may seem: Budget models need to be institution-specific and contextual. For similar reasons, Washington University in St. Louis budgeted and managed its Medicine and Law Schools as "reserve schools" responsible for their own revenues and expenses since the 1960s.

Another mixed model is UCLA, where schools are mocked up in RCM format each year as key context for what is basically a direct expense base approach to budget development. Thus, school-allocated revenues can influence direct expense allocations, but there is no operational devolution of revenues and the right to act upon them.

NOT TO BE CONFUSED WITH RCM

An extreme form of decentralization, *ETOB, or Each Tub on its Own Bottom,* is likely a precursor to RCM but differs materially. Within ETOB universities, schools (the tubs) truly "stand alone" financially and most often academically. They own 100% of their revenues, contain their own comprehensive central administrations, and may even run their own financial accounting systems. With so much decentralization, there is little central administration to allocate. As a senior financial officer at Harvard told one of us in the early 1990s, "To put a budget together for the university, one simply stapled together the budgets from the schools (tubs) and carried them off to the corporation meeting."

In contrast, RCM features shared ownership of revenues, which forces shared investment in strategic thrusts. It also allocates central facilities and administrative costs, thus invoking conversations about the relative balance between central and local services. In this sense, RCM as designed by the University of Pennsylvania in the 1970s was a new balancing model, as much a pulling back from the excess decentralization of the ETOB model as it was a moving away from its then current excess centralization. Compared with RCM universities, ETOB universities look a lot like holding companies.

CHAPTER TWO

The Essential Benefit of RCM: Coupling Responsibility and Authority

Few enterprises in our society are more innately decentralized than colleges and universities. The traditions of collegial governance have deep roots, with the school/department/program structure being almost universal. Faculty members have authority over hires, promotions, fires, program design and production, admission requirements, research foci, quality control, and most expenses. By virtue of tenure, they are strongly vested in the success of their institutions but typically as seen from a departmental perspective.

Yet with all their authority and independence, faculty members do not always exercise appropriate financial responsibility to their institutions. Indeed, more often than not and by "design," financial consequences of academic decisions are not understood at the academic department or school level: Financial responsibility is decoupled from academic choices. Thus, what is best—in fact what is feasible—for institutions as a whole may not be the sum of what is best for individual departments.

In the broadest terms, RCM completes the authority/responsibility circle around affinity groups of disciplines. It gives faculty specific, measurable incentives to exercise their considerable authority *responsibly* for the benefit of themselves, their students, their organizational units, and the institution as a whole. With the right incentives, faculty can become advocates for change and actions they might normally resist when advocated by others—especially central administrators.

In simple mechanistic terms, RCM completes the circle by allocating revenues to schools in exchange for the responsibility for living within them; it couples the costs of facilities and central services to their primary beneficiaries through allocation of indirect costs; and it connects local with central authority, and hence strategies, through the mechanism of subvention.

STRONGER LINKS

One of RCM's great strengths is coupling areas that are often de-coupled within colleges and universities. It connects:

- Academic authority over teaching and research programs (a university's basic products) with responsibility for the resources they generate (sales) and consume by allocating revenues and indirect expenses to academic units.

- Revenues with the primary costs of generating them (in schools and departments), which enables faculty and administrators to better understand—and manage—cause and effect.

- Authority and entrepreneurship of local units, each specific to a discipline or profession, with central authority and university-wide strategy through competition for subvention. This creates a dynamic tension between what's best for local units and what's best for the institution as a whole.

Exhibit A shows the key differences between traditional centrally budgeted and managed universities and an RCM approach. In the central model, all revenues flow into a central "general fund" and then are allocated as expense budgets to academic and administrative units. By contrast the RCM diagram emphasizes the primacy of the schools and colleges in generating, and hence owning, their revenue; those revenues and their attendant direct expenses are coupled in the center box. The schools and colleges also fill and draw from the subvention pool and fund the central administrative units whose services they use.

EXHIBIT A
ILLUSTRATIVE RCM FUND FLOWS

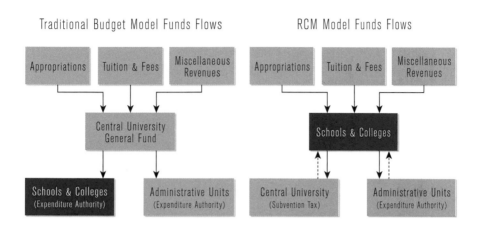

Traditional Budget Model Funds Flows

Appropriations | Tuition & Fees | Miscellaneous Revenues

Central University General Fund

Schools & Colleges (Expenditure Authority) | Administrative Units (Expenditure Authority)

RCM Model Funds Flows

Appropriations | Tuition & Fees | Miscellaneous Revenues

Schools & Colleges

Central University (Subvention Tax) | Administrative Units (Expenditure Authority)

COUPLING ACADEMIC AUTHORITY WITH FINANCIAL RESPONSIBILITY

With RCM, for example, a school of engineering in a large university would own, or keep, tuition revenues generated by engineering class enrollments and the research generated by engineering faculty members—including indirect costs recoveries. In exchange, the engineering school would budget expenses—including indirect costs—within its revenue envelope and actively manage revenue ups and downs. When tuition revenue increases, the school hires faculty and adds new course sections; when tuition revenue decreases, it scales back recruitment and reduces sections and numbers of teaching assistants. When research volume (revenues) go up, the school plans for new space and pays for it with incremental indirect cost recovery; when research volume goes down, the school yields space to other academic departments, thus reducing its indirect cost allocation. Both of these examples couple choice and consequence.

Local ownership of revenues can also yield progress toward institutional goals. Take, for example, the related goals of improving undergraduate teaching and making timely progress to degree. When tuition revenues are allocated to the courses where students enroll, it is easy to see that undergraduate enrollment in large lower-division core courses represents a major source of revenue—especially net revenue, after costs—for most schools and programs. The best way to increase that revenue is to offer the courses students need and to improve the quality of teaching. By increasing revenue, faculty members achieve greater latitude to increase numbers of colleagues, improve working conditions, and even increase compensation, thereby connecting self-interests and institutional priorities.

COUPLING THE COSTS OF ADMINISTRATIVE SERVICES WITH THE PRIMARY CONSUMERS

By explicitly allocating the costs of facilities and administrative services to the revenue-producing centers, RCM provides information on full program costs while encouraging attention to the quality and efficient production of these services. Indeed, if centers must use their revenues to pay for these services, they can—and should—use cost-allocation information to challenge the purveyors (vendors).

But continual scrutiny is required to keep costs low and service quality high. Left to their own devices, even academic administrators tend to forget that administrative services exist to support the academic mission, not self-defined ends. Inattention can beget internal monopolistic behaviors. Focus on and encouragement of constructive tension between the central service suppliers and the responsibility centers—the customers—are necessary to realize the full benefits of identifying and charging indirect costs.

SUBVENTION AND THE COUPLING OF CENTRAL AND LOCAL AUTHORITY AND RESPONSIBILITY

Developing, protecting, and wisely using centrally owned revenues—subventions—contribute to RCM's financial and academic success. Because RCM works better when all centers are dependent on at least some subvention, several universities have imposed revenue taxes to enlarge the subvention pool.

The University of Pennsylvania, for example, considers 20 percent of undergraduate tuition revenues as "university tuition" and allocates that amount to its subvention pool. Penn also charges a 10.5% "participation fee" on indirect cost recoveries. Such taxes explicitly recognize that both the institution and the individual responsibility centers attract students and research dollars. On the other hand, Texas Tech University forgoes a general revenue tax on all centers in favor of a specific negative subvention to only one college.

Subventions help achieve institutional goals, as well as contribute to local goals, thus making the whole greater than the sum of the parts. More specifically, subventions:

- Enable presidents and provosts to compensate for the wide disparities in unit costs of different academic programs that have equivalent quality and typically charge the same tuition unit price (or receive the same per-student state support).

- Serve as incentives by rewarding the development and execution of sound academic plans. Allocations of subvention are made in proportion to a plan's success and alignment with the institution's mission.

- Provide start-up funds for promising new academic ventures. It is crucial, however, that the allocation of these start-up funds not be prescribed by formula.

- Create a focal point in budget proposals for testing school's discipline- or profession-specific goals and university-wide goals to bring them into appropriate consonance.

A CORPORATE COROLLARY

The decentralized structure of RCM bears a strong resemblance to the profit center model of many modern for-profit corporations, particularly conglomerates and multinationals. The two environments share many similar, if not identical, reasons for decentralization.

One fundamental difference exists, however. In the for-profit world, by definition, maximizing profit or shareholder value is the objective. Other issues, such as ethical behavior, societal contributions, and employee satisfaction become constraints. In the university world, the objective is maximizing "academic profit"—typically measured in terms of achieving the university mission through instruction, knowledge development, and service. Finance, namely providing the necessary resources in a sustainable fashion, is both enabler and constraint.

STRATEGIC CONNECTIONS

Inspired in part by financial challenges, higher education has increased its emphasis on the development and execution of strategic plans. Still, too many plans wind up gathering dust because they primarily focus on laudable objectives but give relatively little thought to the resource development and reallocations required to fund implementation.

RCM can be a powerful facilitator of strategic implementation. When developed with the full kit of RCM tools, each annual budget becomes the implementation plan for the next year of the strategic plan. Over the life of a strategic plan, adjustments to markets and economic times are facilitated through distributed ownership of revenues; both success and adaptation are structurally distributed. Thus, academic authority over strategy is coupled with the financial responsibility to deliver.

More specifically:

- Provosts and presidents can challenge deans to develop revenue plans to achieve their schools' and the university's strategic goals.

- Adjusting center expense budgets up or down as center revenues vary is simply a very direct form of natural reallocation.

- Redirection of subventions (or indirect revenue) toward strategic university-wide goals becomes a form of intentional collaboration and/or reallocation.

- Deans' pressures on central administration to deliver better service for less cost can yield another source of strategic funding.

RCM is often described as "letting the schools run on their own." This description overlooks the importance of central steering in viable decentralization—and, no, that is not a contradiction in terms. The academic and financial successes of a university *as a whole* are the responsibility of the president, provost, CFO, and governing board. They need enough overall financial and directional authority to achieve that. Authority commensurate with responsibility applies at the top of the university as well as within individual units.

To be clear, RCM itself does not manage the university. Rather, RCM is a logical representation of the resources available and the expenditures made in managing the university's education, research, and service missions in view of its priorities and objectives. Deans, center directors, and department chairs do the actual hands-on management within policies established by the trustees/regents and central resource allocations and reallocations made by the president and provost. Although much of RCM's language is financial, its values are academic and its public obligations are paramount.

THE COUPLING OF FINANCIAL REALITIES WITH POLITICAL INTERPRETATIONS: GREATER TRANSPARENCY

Anyone with experience in universities knows of the tension endemic among academics and administrators. This tension becomes constructive when an RCM system reveals facts that may challenge (or confirm) lore: Who is really making money and why? Who is subsidizing whom—and why? Why are indirect costs so large relative to expenses in the academic units?

The transparency that RCM encourages—but does not guarantee—may be one of its greatest benefits. While RCM does not expect all colleges and programs to deliver "profits," or positive operating margins, they all are expected to operate within an agreed-upon financial frame determined through revenue ownership and subvention agreements. Such agreements should be based, in part, on centers' contributions to the university's mission and strategic objectives—and be explicitly communicated.

Moreover, the colleges and other revenue-generating centers know exactly what they're paying for administrative and facility-related services. And the providers of those services understand that not only will the colleges know what they are paying but also be able to compare external prices for the same services. Transparency and constructive tension are furthered when universities make public (at least within themselves) comprehensive unit budgets with clear resource redistributions, as exhibited by relative subventions or net operating margins.

We close this chapter on a philosophical note. Alan Wolfe (1996) has suggested that one consequence of natural university decentralization is that "... the university is not an entity with a common purpose, or at least organized around a system-defining core." He then goes on to claim this decentralization in combination with the institution of tenure "... explains the failures of faculty self-governance." We take a somewhat different view, more in line with Michael Cohen's and James March's (1986) characterization of universities as "organized anarchies," and argue that decentralized authority and competing, often inconsistent goals—indeed, the lack of a "system-defining core"—are in the very nature of universities. They are realities to be reckoned with rather than pathologies to be lamented. We argue that reformulating and formalizing this natural decentralization in the management structure and incentives of an institution can not only mitigate the negative effects of decoupling of responsibility from authority, but also enable and accentuate the positive attributes of decentralization.

CHAPTER THREE

An RCM Primer: Design, Structure, and Complexities

This chapter delves into the details behind a prototypical responsibility center budget, followed by a more in-depth explanation of the complexities associated with designing and managing an RCM system.

RCM 1.0: THE BASICS

Table 1 illustrates a prototypical responsibility center budget format for a university with two schools, A and B, and a central administration. The table shows each school's ownership of revenues and indirect expenses. It also exhibits the concepts of participation and subvention: Participation here is a 20% tax on unrestricted revenues; subvention is the distribution or return of the tax proceeds along with any other revenues "owned" by central administration. The table also introduces the term, "indirect revenues," the algebraic sum of participation and subvention; indirect revenue is the same as the net operating margin of the units shown.

TABLE 1
RESPONSIBILITY CENTER FORMAT ($000,000)
PROTOTYPICAL UNIVERSITY

	Academic Centers		Administrative Centers	Total
	School A	School B		
Direct Revenue				
Tuition	120	60	0	180
Financial Aid	(20)	(10)	0	(30)
Endowment & Gifts				
Unrestricted	0	0	25	25
Restricted	30	50	0	80
Research				
Restricted	100	200	0	300
Indirect Cost Recovery (F&A)	30	60	0	90
Indirect Revenue				
Participation	(26)	(22)	48	0
Subvention	38	35	(73)	0
Total Revenues	272	373	0	645
Direct Expenditures				
Instruction	100	67	0	167
Research	100	200	0	300
Facilities	0	0	108	108
Administration	0	0	70	70
Indirect Expenditures				
Facilities (square feet)	42	66	(108)	0
Administration (expenditures)	30	40	(70)	0
Total Expenditures	272	373	0	645

Here are some details underlying the numbers in each line and column.

Revenues

Tuition. Tuition revenues are allocated in proportion to credit hours taught. School A generates 67% of total credit hours (120/180) and School B generates 33% (60/180). An alternative algorithm might give the majoring school some direct portion of tuition revenues to represent the fact that it attracted the student's interest (and tuition payments) and incurs advising costs. In that case, the university might allocate 80% percent of total tuition revenues in proportion to credit hours generated and 20% in proportion to total numbers of registered majors. Algorithms governing ownership of graduate tuition revenues sometimes differ from those for undergraduate tuition. As an example, significantly larger fractions of doctoral or professional student tuition may be allocated to the majoring school to reflect the intensive mentoring that characterizes that higher level of study.

Undergraduate Institutional Financial Aid. Typically this would be allocated in proportion to tuition revenues to recognize that the institution, rather the centers, sets undergraduate aid policy. In some cases, aid is summed across students in individual courses, with the net revenues allocated to the course and hence to the teaching center. (This approach, however, penalizes schools that attract and teach needy students.) In accordance with contemporary accounting principles, aid would be subtracted from gross tuition. In Table 1, financial aid totaling $30 million is distributed to Schools A and B in the same ratio as their tuition revenues.

Endowment & Gifts. Here, unrestricted endowments and gifts belong to the central administration and fill the subvention pool. Restricted gifts belong to the centers.

Research. Faculty principal investigators in the individual schools A and B own direct research expenses. Indirect cost recovery (F&A) is allocated to the schools whose faculty members have the grants and contracts. Recoveries belong with the schools that incur, and are allocated, the indirect costs of doing research.

Participation. Table 1 shows a "participation" charge (tax) of 20% of unrestricted center revenues available to fill the subvention pool. Funds flow from centers A and B into the administration center, where they are added to centrally owned endowment and gifts to form a subvention pool of $73 million.

Subvention. This refers to a discretionary allocation of general institutional revenues, including the proceeds from participation. Subvention allocations balance the impacts of different unit costs among diverse academic programs—historical, intrinsic, or desired—and fund institutional priorities. Table 1 shows a subvention pool of $73 million, with $38 million allocated to academic center A and $35 million to center B. School A might rank higher in the priority pecking order, with its $38 million subvention; or its unit costs might be higher.

Indirect revenue. In Table 1, indirect revenue is the algebraic sum of participation and subvention. Here's another way to look at this: Indirect revenue is the net operating margin of each unit. For center A, this is $12 million; for B, $13 million. Some would argue that indirect revenue is a subsidy, and therefore B is more subsidized than A. This becomes a valid argument only when administrative indirect cost allocations are "perfect" and unit prices reflect unit costs.

Direct Expenses

Direct expenditures for instruction, research, facilities and administration are simple and straightforward. If a school finances part or all of a major renovation or a new building, debt service would be included in direct expenses as a line item.

Indirect Expenses

Facilities. This category comprises utilities, repair and maintenance, custodial service, interest on related debt, and depreciation (or a substitute, such as 2% of replacement costs). Utility metering and detailed occupancy and maintenance cost data allow for accurate allocation of facilities expenses to responsibility centers. With sufficient data, facilities could be direct expenses in A's and B's budgets—just as if the schools were renting appropriate space from an outside landlord.

Administration. Each administrative center is functionally aligned to serve multiple clients: student services, enrollment management, human resources, financial administration, research administration, and information technology services, to name the most common. These functions have multiple drivers or usage measures.

Student services, for example, might be allocated in proportion to majors or credit hours generated in a center. In that case, the university would measure usage. Information technology central costs may be allocated in proportion to the number of faculty, staff, and students in a center; allocations are done in proportion to access. Human resources costs are usually allocated in proportion to employees served in each center. Research administration is allocated in proportion to total numbers of contracts and grants or total dollar levels of research (or a weighted average of both) in an attempt to estimate transaction volume. With more centralized, less direct services, such as the controller's office, allocation is typically in proportion to a center's total expenses.

For ease of illustration, Table 1 lumps together all administrative expenses and uses total direct expenses as the basis for allocation. Center A has direct expenses of $200 million, while B has $267 million. The administrative costs of $70 million are allocated proportionally to direct expenses: $30 million to A, $40 million to B.

Knowing the way Table 1 is structured, we now expand it to show RCM in action. Table 2 compares budgets with actual revenue and expense performances. Note that School A exceeds its tuition budget by $10 million and its indirect cost recovery (F&A) by $2 million; at the 20% participation rate, it supplies $2 million more than planned to the subvention pool; thus the school realizes $10 million more in total revenues than budgeted (planned). School A spends $2 million more in instruction than planned to cover additional teaching costs. Combining this overage with the revenue increment, we see an overall surplus of $8 million, which is added to the beginning-year fund balance to yield an end-of-year balance of $10 million. *School A retains its operating surplus to deploy in future years.*

School B fares less well. Its revenues fall short of budget by $7 million, reducing the participation obligation by $1 million and resulting in a total revenue shortfall of $6 million, while efforts to compensate during the year by reducing expenses offset this decrement by only $2 million. School B's ending-year balance is now a negative $4 million. *B is obligated to repay this amount in future years' budgets.*

Central administrative costs also vary between budgets and actuals, but because schools cannot intervene to manage these during a year, the budgeted levels are typically "guaranteed" as the levels against which school bottom-line performances are calculated.

TABLE 2
RESPONSIBILITY CENTER FORMAT ($000,000)
PROTOTYPICAL UNIVERSITY

	School A		School B		Administrative Centers		Total	
	Budget	Actual	Budget	Actual	Budget	Actual	Budget	Actual
Revenue								
Tuition	120	130	60	58	0	0	180	188
Financial Aid	(20)	(20)	(10)	(10)	0	0	(30)	(30)
Endowment & Gifts								
Unrestricted	0	0	0	0	25	25	25	25
Restricted	30	30	50	50	0	0	80	80
Research								
Restricted	100	100	200	200	0	0	300	300
Indirect Cost Recovery (F&A)	30	32	60	55	0	0	90	87
Participation	(26)	(28)	(22)	(21)	48	49	0	0
Subvention	38	38	35	35	(73)	(73)	0	0
Total Revenues	272	282	373	367	0	1	645	650
Direct Expenditures								
Instruction	100	102	67	65	0	0	167	167
Research	100	100	200	200	0	0	300	300
Facilities	0	0	0	0	150	150	150	150
Administration	0	0	0	0	100	100	100	100
Indirect Expenditures								
Facilities (square feet)	42	42	66	66	(150)	(150)	(42)	(42)
Administration (expenditures)	30	30	40	40	(100)	(100)	(30)	(30)
Total Expenditures	272	274	373	371	0	0	645	645
Surplus/(Deficit)	0	8	0	(4)	0	1	0	5
Beginning Fund Balance*		2		2		0		4
Surplus/Deficit		8		(4)		1		5
Ending Fund Balance*		10		(2)		1		9
	26.0	28.4	22.0	20.6	0.0	0.0	48.0	49.0

*Fund balances are often called "inter-center bank balance"

TIES TO BEST PRACTICES

RCM, simply through its budget format, exemplifies several best practices in budgeting:

The All-Funds Approach. Too often, only unrestricted sources, sometimes known as the "general fund," are discussed during budget development. With an all-funds approach, however, the deans' budget proposals would describe not only how they plan to expend their and the university's unrestricted (general fund) sources but also include planned uses of endowment distributions, projected gift flows, one-time deployments of fund balances (including carry-forwards), and planned transfers from operations to planned funds for future renovations. The all-funds approach has obvious strengths: Everyone sees the big picture, and the ability to amass multiple resources to support major initiatives is vastly enhanced.

Table 2 exhibits both central and school-restricted endowment and gift revenues, as well as the (restricted) direct expenses for research. A more detailed table—perhaps with columns for each school for unrestricted and restricted revenues *and* expenses and with a breakdown of expenses into faculty and staff salaries—would show even more, such as the dependence of salaries on endowments, gifts, and research grants as a risk assessment, for example. Table 2 also shows beginning balances for School A, School B, and the university and how those balances change based on the schools' actual financial performances. In particular, for the next year's budget, School A is entitled to use some of its accumulated balance of $11 million, and School B must begin repayment of its $2 million balance sheet deficit.

Transparency. At one end of the spectrum are opaque universities, in which local units generate and control most information. The institutional social norm emphasizes that information is power according to who owns it, not who uses it. At the other extreme are transparent universities, which favor widespread distribution of and access to information. Their social norm is global usage: Information is power according to how much there is, how relevant and accurate it is, and how well it is used to support decision making.

Table 2, if broadly distributed and understood within both School A and School B, would reveal each school's revenues and total costs, the total costs of facilities and administrative services in the university, the schools' consumption of these services, the differences between participation contributed and subvention received, how well each school managed its actual financial performance during the fiscal year, and how much each school "has in the bank." A comprehensive budget format is, indeed, worth a thousand words.

Of course, openness can bring its own problems. If decisions are known, but not considered grounded in reliable data or reached through clear and compelling priorities, people will engage in second-guessing and invidious comparisons. But that happens anyway in opaque systems, which offer few data to disabuse people of their misconceptions.

Multi-Year Planning. Most universities consider only the next year during budget development. Some go to five years or beyond, although it's hard to see that far ahead except with respect to capital planning. In general, multiple-year purviews are preferable, both going forward and backward in time.

Going forward captures most academic initiatives, development of attendant funding, and capital construction plans that require long lead times. Looking backward infuses the budget process with memories of prior years' decisions and the considerations on which they were based. For example, if expanded to include prior years' actuals, resulting fund balances, and forecasted growth or draw down of fund balances, Table 2 would show additional changes in the balance sheet, plus its relationship to operations—and provide even more transparency.

RCM 2.0: THE NITTY-GRITTY

In real life, RCM is much more complex than Table 2's rounded-off numbers for two colleges and two administrative units. Moving from such a simplistic model to a practical model would require steps such as:

- Expanding the number of colleges and schools, perhaps reaching 20 responsibility centers.
- Adding auxiliary units (housing, dining, bookstore, parking, athletics), and possibly research centers and institutes, as responsibility centers.
- Adding all relevant administrative centers.
- Bringing all funds into the model and ensuring that revenue and expense categories align with the definitions used in the institution's published financial statements.
- Addressing the complexities of restricted and unrestricted funds.
- Allowing for internal transfers, both among responsibility centers and among responsibility centers and administrative and support units.
- Allowing for the selective collection of revenues by administrative and support units.
- Providing added transparency with respect to cost pools and their respective drivers.
- Filling and allocating the subvention pool to recognize unit costs and university-wide priorities.
- Developing policies that govern access to and repayment of year-end surpluses and deficits.

In addition, an institution's unique characteristics, policies, and agreements would need to be reviewed, revised, and appropriately reflected in its RCM model.

Table 3 illustrates the fund flows, allocation rules, cost pools, and drivers of an actual RCM model (minus some of the institution's centers and with variations in the numbers to protect the source). Like Table 2, it arrays the responsibility centers across the top of the page, with the rows revealing each center's revenues and expenses. But Table 3 has some immediately noticeable changes. For example, restricted and unrestricted funds have been distinguished for each center and with respect to each direct line item. The revenue and expense categories have been expanded to include those portrayed in the institution's annual financial statements. Also, the participation fees, subvention, and indirect revenues have been moved to the bottom of the report.

Starting at the top left of Table 3, we note that other modifications include the following:

Driver Column. The second column on the report offers a driver code, which indicates how each line item is allocated across the responsibility centers. The first five rows all contain the code "SCH," meaning the revenues are distributed to centers based on their proportional share of student credit hours. In Row 6, "R&I" stands for research and instruction, indicating an algorithm for state appropriations. The line items coded with "D" represent direct allocations. Other codes refer to student headcount (HCS), direct expenses (EXP), total headcount (HCT), net assignable square feet (SQFT), and research expenses (RES).

Other Column. Just to the right of the Auxiliaries heading is a column simply titled "Other." Real RCM scenarios typically have a set of revenues generated by administrative and support units that cannot be reasonably allocated to responsibility centers. These are usually one-off items, such as a research grant secured by the library that should be kept separate. Because these revenues accrue to administrative and support units, they reduce the expense budgets of the units prior to their allocation.

Restricted and Unrestricted Funds. The expanded detail with respect to restricted and unrestricted funds helps illustrate the full scope of resources employed on behalf of each center's mission. In Table 3, the restricted funds have expenses greater than revenues in each instance, creating unit margin losses (Row 25). This indicates that each college is using unrestricted funds to subsidize programs that are funded through restricted revenues.

Indirect Expenses. The allocation of indirect expenses begins on Row 27. This shows five cost pools: Academic, Executive, Administrative, Facilities, and Research. In the column immediately to the right of each pool is a rate, which indicates the basis on which the indirect costs are attributed to each center. For example, the academic pool is allocated based on student headcount (HCS) at a rate of $1,444 per student. The executive pool is allocated based on direct expenses (EXP) at a rate of $0.026 per dollar, or 2.6% of total direct expenses. These per-unit rates are valuable, rapid estimations of the net resources available from proposed new opportunities—but remember they are average and not marginal rates. Rates should change each year, as the cost pool budgets change based on need and institutional strategy and as the allocation bases change across units. For example, increased headcount may not lead to an increase in allocated administrative costs; therefore, administrative unit costs would simply decline from the current rate of $1,207 per person.

Cost Drivers. Rows 42 through 46 illustrate the driver frequency for each of the cost pools. For example, each center has a listing of student headcount. These drivers are used to determine each center's proportional share allocation. While this model uses five drivers, complex RCM models commonly use eight to 12 drivers. Because a great deal of risk is associated with using too many cost drivers, models employing more than 12 drivers are rare.

Indirect Expense Allocations. A distribution of cost to the centers appears in the columns next to the indirect costs (Rows 26 – 32). This is simply the multiplication of each pool's per-unit rate by each center's driver. Table 3 uses total driver values to allocate costs to centers—for example, the EXP driver involves the sum of unrestricted and restricted expenses—but the allocations appear in the unrestricted column. This represents somewhat of a compromise because headcounts, for example, are not always simple to apportion between fund types.

Fully-Costed Margin. As seen in Row 35, two of the four centers—Business and Liberal Arts— have a positive fully costed margin. Medicine's margin is negative, with Auxiliaries in sum positive. Positive or negative margin can often be attributed to the college's business model and cost of instructional delivery. On the other hand, its market or market penetration may be weak, its enrollment too low, its pricing strategy in need of revising, or its costs too high. Further analyses are required to address the matter. Following the margin line to the far right, this budget predicts that the institution as a whole will deliver a $489,000 surplus.

Participation Fee. Rows 37 and 38 indicate each center's required participation fee and subvention/indirect revenue distribution. Row 37 shows that each center pays 18% of total unrestricted sources. Even after paying participation, however, both the College of Business and the College of Liberal Arts have positive fully costed margins of $332,000 and $220,000, respectively. Consequently, these two colleges do not receive allocations from the subvention fund on Row 38. Or, to put it another way, they could receive small negative subventions.

On the other hand, the College of Medicine exhibits a $33.8 million negative fully costed margin. The total column of Row 37 indicates that the institution

TABLE 3
ILLUSTRATIVE RCM MODEL

#	Driver	($000s)	Rate	Business Unrest	Business Restricted	Business Total	Liberal Arts Unrest	Liberal Arts Restricted	Liberal Arts Total	Medicine Unrest	Medicine Restricted	Medicine Total	Auxiliaries Unrest	Auxiliaries Restricted	Auxiliaries Total	Other Total	Model Total
1		**Revenue**															
2	SCH	Tuition		$27,265	$0	$27,265	$111,999	$0	$111,999	$44,207	$0	$44,207	$0	$0	$0	$55	$183,526
3	SCH	Scholarships		(4,115)	(553)	(4,689)	(24,149)	(850)	(24,999)	(10,454)	(902)	(11,356)	-	-	-	(1,145)	(42,169)
4	SCH	Waivers		(1,473)	-	(1,473)	(9,184)	-	(9,184)	(1,321)	-	(1,321)	-	-	-	-	(11,978)
5	SCH	Student Fees		3,732	-	3,732	15,149	-	15,149	3,797	-	3,797	1,738	-	1,738	2,735	27,151
6	R&J	State Appropriations		9,997	-	9,997	64,983	-	64,983	49,987	-	49,987	-	-	-	-	124,966
7	D	Sponsored Activities		-	1,574	1,574	-	11,883	11,883	63,288	132,521	195,809	-	55	55	10,725	220,047
8	D	F&A Cost Recovery		106	-	106	3,616	-	3,616	28,187	-	28,187	-	-	-	1,953	33,863
9	D	Gifts		151	32	183	547	818	1,365	3,060	1,955	5,015	1,404	99	1,502	2,488	103,553
10	D	Sales and Services		97	-	97	160	3	163	1,757	128	1,885	32,006	-	32,006	3,264	37,413
11	D	Investment Income		0	317	317	5	1,471	1,476	3	5,231	5,233	3	108	112	3,497	10,636
12	D	Other & Transfers		(200)	81	(119)	788	203	990	1,673	860	2,533	(10,260)	-	(10,260)	-	(6,856)
13		**Total Revenues**		**$35,560**	**$1,451**	**$37,011**	**$163,913**	**$13,528**	**$177,441**	**$184,183**	**$139,793**	**$323,976**	**$24,890**	**$262**	**$25,153**	**$23,573**	**$587,153**
14																	
15		**Direct Expenses**															
16	D	Salaries and Wages		$13,381	$1,038	$14,419	$55,754	$6,780	$62,534	$107,432	$60,095	$167,527	$6,910	$222	$7,132	$0	$251,611
17	D	Fringe Benefits		3,478	172	3,650	15,561	1,418	16,979	29,380	16,081	45,460	1,851	61	1,913	-	68,002
18	D	Admin. & Facility		0	-	0	63	54	117	5,220	28,786	34,006	759	3,000	3,759	-	37,883
19	D	Equipment		9	-	9	2,036	2,071	4,107	1,341	2,141	3,482	41	-	41	-	7,640
20	D	Services & Contracts		240	215	455	2,647	1,042	3,689	16,844	26,247	43,091	8,385	273	8,658	-	55,894
21	D	Supplies		610	174	784	3,987	1,528	5,515	5,019	7,109	12,128	2,124	5	2,129	-	20,556
22	D	Other		350	75	425	29	979	1,009	2,918	4,676	7,594	317	4	321	-	9,348
23		**Total Direct Expenses**		**$18,069**	**$1,574**	**$19,743**	**$80,077**	**$13,872**	**$93,949**	**$166,153**	**$145,135**	**$313,289**	**$20,388**	**$565**	**$23,953**	**$0**	**$450,934**
24																	
25		**Unit Margin**		$17,490	($223)	$17,268	$83,836	($345)	$83,492	$16,030	($5,342)	$10,688	$4,502	($3,303)	$1,200	$23,573	$136,220
26																	
27		**Indirect Expenses**	**Rate**														
28	HCS	Academic	$1,444			$4,655			$19,527			$2,277			$0	($3,575)	$30,035
29	EXP	Executive	2.8%			511			2,430			8,105			620	(2,145)	13,811
30	HCT	Administrative	$1,207			4,331			18,174			4,594			204	(5,482)	32,784
31	SQFT	Facilities	$24.86			933			12,840			16,397			2,276	(7,150)	39,595
32	RES	Research	6.7%			105			796			13,119			4	(5,462)	19,506
33		**Total Unit Allocations**				$10,535			$53,767			$44,492			$3,104	($23,833)	$135,731
34																	
35		**Fully Costed Margin**				$6,733			$29,724			($33,804)			($1,904)		**$489**
36																	
37		Participation Fee (18%)				(6,401)			(29,504)			(33,153)			(4,480)		(73,538)
38		Internal Revenue Distribution				-			-			66,957			6,384		73,341
39		**Year End Carryforward**				**$332**			**$220**			**$0**			**$0**		**$686**
40																	
41		**Drivers**															
42	HCS	Total Student Headcount				3,224			13,523			1,577			-		
43	EXP	Total Direct Expenditures				19,743			93,949			313,289			23,953		
44	HCT	Total Headcount				3,588			15,057			3,806			169		
45	SQFT	Net Assignable Square Feet				37,530			516,482			659,554			91,559		
46	RES	Total Direct Research				1,574			11,883			195,809			55		

will collect $73.5 million in participation fees. After paying $33 million to the subvention pool, Medicine requires almost $67 million in subvention to balance. Similarly, after the attribution of indirect costs and payment of participation fees, auxiliary operations are projecting a loss, requiring that indirect revenues of $6.3 million be allocated to ensure breakeven operations.

Institution Margin & Strategic Initiative Funding. The overall institution margin is projected at a positive $489,000. Rows 37 and 38 also indicate that the institution can collect $73.5 million in participation fees and distribute only $73.3 million in institutional revenues. The positive subvention fund balance of $197,000 provides additional resources for the central administration. Ultimately, adding the institutional margin and the subvention fund margin together indicates that the institution has $686,000 of available funds. The leadership team can use these funds at its discretion, presumably for strategic initiatives— one of which may be booking a positive margin to enhance fiscal stability.

The numbers that emerge in an RCM model often result in more questions than answers. Regarding Table 3, for example, why does the College of Medicine require such a large distribution of indirect revenue? Is there a way to make the College of Business and the College of Liberal Arts less dependent on tuition? How is the College of Medicine operating with such a low proportion of direct expenses allocated to salaries? What central academic services justify an overhead charge of $1,444 per student? (See Chapter 7 for a discussion of the analyses that RCM enables.)

Note that Table 3 shows administrative centers pre-aggregated into functional indirect cost pools rather than placed in the same natural-classification detail as academic centers. A more comprehensive, transparent presentation would show the budgets of the major administrative centers in columns alongside and in the same natural classifications as those for the direct centers, and then allocate each according to the rules governing the pool to which it belongs.

◤ MANAGEMENT MAXIMS

In the early 1980s, when the University of Southern California developed what became Revenue Center Management, it enunciated a set of broad organizational principles to guide deliberations and ultimately shape the new system. These principles, as elaborated upon by John R. Curry in *Resource Allocation in Higher Education* (The University of Michigan Press, 1996), enable tests of various approaches to organizational design and budget-rule specification. In particular, each component of budget system design, both current and proposed, can be put to this test: Where is there consistency—and inconsistency—with these maxims? Design continues until the institution arrives at reasonably uniform consonance.

- The closer the decision maker is to the relevant information, the better the decision is likely to be. (If you are too far removed from the action, you don't know enough to make a decision, and even if you do, you are too remote to implement it.)

- The degree of decentralization of an organization should be proportional to its size and complexity. (Management scope should be limited to what you can understand and do.)

- Responsibility should be commensurate with authority, and vice versa. (Those who have the power to act should know the consequences and be responsible for them.)

- The central administration should retain sufficient academic and fiscal leverage to ensure achievement of institutional goals. (Local optimization does not always lead to globally optimal outcomes.)

- Clear rewards and sanctions are required to make the distribution of responsibility and authority operational, as well as to effect their coupling. (If no one wins or loses when things go right or wrong, no one is responsible.)

- Resource-expanding incentives are preferable to resource-dividing rules. (Entrepreneurs are more fun than tax lawyers.)

- Successful decentralization requires common information systems that provide local and central managers with timely and accurate performance reports. (Dueling data dilute responsibility and give rise to finger pointing.)

- Outcome measures are preferable to input (process) controls. (Delivery, not control, is the goal.)

- Achievement of academic excellence requires that academic performance criteria be explicit and, where possible, quantified (lest financial currency drive out academic currency.)

- Stable financial environments facilitate good planning. (Rapid fluctuations in resources play havoc with education and research.)

- People play better games when they own the rules. (In an organized anarchy, why should you play by other anarchists' rules?)

KEY DECISIONS

Designing an RCM model like the one presented in Table 3 requires at least eight critical decisions. The first four create the basic structure of any RCM model; the last four relate to revenue and cost algorithms.

1. Categorization of Units. Categorizing each operating unit as either a responsibility center or an administrative service center determines the model's structure. At first glance, this may appear relatively simple; however, debate typically swirls around the units for which strong cases can be made either way, including graduate schools, honors colleges, undergraduate colleges, and centers and institutes. Some institutions develop hybrids. To reduce public criticism for using subvention support for core facilities such as libraries and museums, for example, the University of Pennsylvania created resource centers—a category between a traditional responsibility center and an administrative service center.

2. Scope of Revenues. Adopting an all-funds approach to budgeting provides the most benefits. This decision must be made early in the model's design.

3. Number and Categorization of Cost Pools. Exhibiting every administrative center as an allocable cost provides transparency although it introduces greater complexity. Aggregating administrative centers into pools with the same allocation drivers makes life simpler, but the simplicity comes at the cost of full transparency. Some degree of aggregation is preferable, although the budgets of each pool component should be available for review in the background.

4. Cost Pool Step-Downs. While the step-down approach to indirect cost allocation may be the reigning standard, it makes simple calculations and comparisons difficult. For example, if attributable space costs are first allocated to student services, and the thus "loaded" student services costs are allocated to schools, the schools cannot calculate the total direct costs of student services by summing allocations across responsibility centers. The University of Southern California addressed this problem by showing the space costs of each administrative center in a separate line. Thus, allocated student services costs would exhibit a "student services-direct" line and a "student services-facilities" line. Such unbundling enhances transparency.

By the same token, if step-downs are eschewed and total facilities costs are allocated to the responsibility centers, say in proportion to the square footage each center occupies, the allocation would not be directly comparable to what each center could lease on the market since it contains the costs of administrative space.

5. Distribution of Tuition. RCM models vary in how they distribute tuition revenues. The variations are driven by two primary decisions.

The first is whether the algorithm for tuition distributions should incorporate a cost of instruction weighting. Tuition weighting attempts to account for the problem of common tuition prices across units with different costs of instruction. Weights carry a lot of power; small changes in them can swing millions of dollars in revenues from one responsibility center to another. Because of this sensitivity, weighting formulas tend to be complex and, consequently, few people understand them. This lack of understanding reduces transparency and can turn weighting formulas into negotiating magnets. Moreover, weighting is almost always based on costs as they are rather than on what they should be. Because weighting factors can help ratify and ossify inefficient models of instruction and hide subsidies, it's best to avoid tuition weighting unless it is already part of the institutional culture through state appropriations (See Case Study 4 in Chapter 5).

Implementing a model without weighting factors appears to put colleges with relatively high instructional costs at a disadvantage, almost ensuring that their fully costed margins will be negative. This is not necessarily bad. Indeed, it is likely when common prices fund disparate costs. As provosts, CFOs, and deans come to understand the business model governing each school, they can better balance high-priority, higher cost programs with subvention harvested from the units having inherently lower costs of instruction. A good test of the legitimacy of the common price/disparate cost approach is to ask deans and admissions directors whether students would pay differential tuitions for the higher cost programs. Note: when weighting factors are involved, what students are *actually* paying in tuition to a school is obscured; the issue of differential tuitions across student markets is accordingly suppressed.

The second major tuition distribution decision relates to how tuition revenues should be shared between the center teaching the course and the center in which the student is enrolled (the student's center of record, or major). Benchmarking this distribution will yield results from 50% to the center of instruction and 50% to the center of record, all the way up to 80% to the center of instruction and 20% to the center of record. Weighting the distribution to the center of instruction is generally warranted because it incurs larger costs by delivering courses. Ideally, the allocation formula should recognize that the majoring center incurs some costs of recruitment and advising, even as new students fulfill core or distribution requirements in other schools, and provide incentives for recruitment of majors. Graduate tuition, for example, is often weighted more heavily to the majoring unit. Dual-degree and hybrid programs can also add complexity to allocation algorithms.

For public universities, the issue is whether to allocate the higher out-of-state tuition per credit hour to the centers where out-of-state students take courses and major. Many universities do this because they are encouraging recruitment and enrollment of more out-of-state students. Others pool in-state and out-of-state tuitions, then determine and allocate a blended amount per credit hour.

6. Distribution of State Appropriations. Public institutions must decide whether and how to distribute state appropriations. Institutions that consider state appropriations as tuition surrogates might reasonably allocate those funds to responsibility centers in proportion to each center's tuition revenues. That characterization, however, has lost favor as research universities have come to understand that research does not cover its full costs and therefore is also being supported by state sources. State appropriations could be allocated in proportion to the sum of research and tuition revenues; more complex formulas might be based on which area the institution wants to grow. It is not uncommon to see state appropriations split, with 20% to 50% allocated in proportion to research and 80% to 50% allocated in proportion to instruction.

Not all institutions allocate appropriations to the centers. Indiana University, the University of Michigan, and the University of Minnesota, for example, retain appropriations centrally as a means of funding the subvention pool. Although this approach has historical precedent—most state universities have long allocated appropriations centrally—states appear likely to continue decreasing their support of public universities. Diversifying the sources of subvention would reduce the likelihood of a large funding shortfall tied to reduced state appropriations.

7. Distribution of Scholarship Costs. Most institutions consider access at the undergraduate level an institutional priority and believe that all centers should equally carry the burden of scholarship costs. Typically, these costs are allocated from a central aid pool, according to the tuition algorithm. While this tends to be the most common approach, models have to account for scholarships belonging to and awarded by schools. These scholarships are usually shown as direct expenses—but should be deductions from revenues—and can supplement or substitute for central awards. Coordination is needed to optimize the benefit of the sum. As graduate tuition discounts, waivers, scholarships, and training grants are typically controlled at the college level, it is common to find them shown as direct expenses in each responsibility center.

8. Distribution of Indirect Cost Recoveries (F&A). RCM models tend to treat indirect cost recoveries (F&A) fairly consistently because these resources are generated by centers and can be easily tracked back to grants held by faculty members in the centers. Because centers are also allocated the indirect costs supporting their restricted programs, the centers need all indirect cost recoveries to offset allocated costs.

Trying to allocate these revenues can complicate the transition to RCM. In many public universities, for example, central research operations and initiatives are funded by a percentage of indirect cost recoveries; these often accrue to vice presidents for research. Similarly, academic departments and principal investigators may receive a share. These situations do not comport with the basic RCM principle of matching revenues with the costs that give rise to them.

In a central system, indirect cost recoveries (F&A) should be understood as offsetting the facilities and administrative costs—mostly central administration, except for departmental administration—that generate them. When those costs are allocated, so should be the revenues generated to recover them. It can be difficult, however, to undo these deals to establish an RCM model.

Public universities often set up foundations to administer research and earmark indirect cost recoveries (F&A) to support the foundations. There is little rationale in any system for supporting such a foundation by indirect cost recoveries (F&A), unless one uses only the "research administration" component of the rate. Research administration budgets should be based on total resources available and desired levels of service to faculty members—just like any other service unit.

CHAPTER FOUR

How RCM Is Working: What the Literature Has to Say

Chapters 1, 2, and 3 taken together provide a relatively comprehensive primer on RCM along with some of our thoughts about strengths and weaknesses compared with alternate approaches to budgeting and financial management. Chapters 4 and 5 expand our scope, especially with respect to the first edition, to include seeing RCM as others see it—the literature review—and seeing RCM up close and from within nine case-study universities. The multiple observations and perspectives selected and elucidated inform Chapter 6 where we reassess promise vs. performance.

For the present chapter, while the list of books and articles presented in the bibliography is relatively long, our review will be relatively short. Indeed, many recent writings evaluate, reprise, and only marginally extend the works of earlier writers and thus enable us to focus on only a few key books and articles.

We have already drawn upon and cited several important sources as we characterized and assessed the strengths and weaknesses of the three basic budgeting models. Moreover, in one way or another, each of the authors of this second edition has been a part of the evolution of incentive-based systems as a student, designer, implementer, practitioner, writer, and consultant about the subject matter. It is, therefore, somewhat difficult to separate contents of literature from our own experiences and internalization of writings of fellow intellectual travelers.

We attempt objectivity nonetheless. In our judgment, the seminal literature on the subject of university budgeting in recent times reached a new high-water mark with the publication of Hopkins and Massy, *Planning Models for Colleges and Universities* (1981). In this path-breaking book, Hopkins and Massy introduced, among other concepts, budget equilibrium, according to which the balancing over time of the growth rates of revenues and expenses becomes more important than annual—one-time—balancing. Further, before the advent of desk-top spreadsheet capabilities, they developed a computer-based, spread-sheet-like planning model that enabled contemplation and development of equilibrium strategies through multi-year projections based on key planning parameters. One might characterize this work as comprising a technological model of budgeting.

As this work was developing in the 1970s, other universities were wrestling with how to respond to the forces that were innately and unintentionally decentralizing their universities. The most structured and explicit response occurred at the University of Pennsylvania, which embarked on what one might call a new organizational and behavioral model of budgeting: a set of business rules and processes that would become a new paradigm, Responsibility Center Management.

While University of Pennsylvania President Martin Meyerson, Vice Provost John Hobstetter, Budget Director Jon Strauss, and Historian Robert Zemsky were the architects and published a variety of papers on the subject, it was Ed Whalen's book, *Responsibility Center Budgeting: An Approach to Decentralized Management for Institutions of Higher Education* (1991) that brought the many aspects of revenue-incentive and full-costing decentralized budget models together. The University of Pennsylvania figured in the content of the book, especially since it was a new Indiana University President Tom Erlich arriving from the University of Pennsylvania who prompted Indiana to move toward RCM, and directed Ed Whalen, Indiana University's budget director at the time, to make RCM happen. Whalen's book drew heavily on the University of Southern California's design, experience, and internal papers on the development of Revenue Center Management, but elucidated and further developed the subject from his perspective as an economist; he included a specific chapter on the University of Southern California's experience with RCM (Curry in Whalen, 1991).

The initiatives at the University of Pennsylvania, University of Southern California, and Indiana University were guided by five time-tested maxims gleaned from the broader management literature about decentralization and reported here as amalgams of those written in Whalen (1991) and Curry in Massy, et al (1996):

- **Proximity** – the closer the decision maker is to the implementation point, the more relevant the information and the better the decision.

- **Proportionality** – the larger and more complex the organization, the more it can benefit from distributed authority and responsibility.

- **Symmetry** – at each level of an organization, responsibility should be commensurate with authority, and vice versa.

- **Operationalization** – clear rewards and sanctions are required to make distributed authority and responsibility work.

- **Knowledge** – the better the information available, the better the decision; the more common the data developed and understood, the better the performance measures and the stronger the accountability.

These maxims continue to be broad-based guides to thinking about how to organize institutions, universities included, and are relatively unchallenged among critics.

Whalen's book and the papers and conversations it reprises and digests constitute rationales for moving toward devolution of revenues, allocation of full costs, and commensurate decentralization of budget authority and responsibility. Later works begin the chronicling of characteristics of successful implementations: In Massy (1996), for example, Curry notes that there may be cultural and exogenous conditions that are necessary for successful management of change: internal discontent about "how (budgetary) things are done around here;" exogenous factors contributing to a sense of fiscal crisis; unrequited ambitions with broadening desires for access to a defined incentive structure; alignment of leadership around new directions; successful pilots of incentive-based deals; and an evolving coalition of like-minded faculty members and deans. Kotter (1996) stresses this last point in his book, *Leading Change.*

Further in Massy, Strauss notes that the *presentation* of departments and divisions at Worcester Polytechnic Institute as revenue responsibility centers and the discussions that ensued led to a gradual and beneficial redistribution of resources. But the overall size and complexity of Worcester Polytechnic's budget, along with a lack of a critical mass of faculty and chairs favoring changes in responsibility for revenues, stalled this initiative, and the processes did not change.

In *Responsibility Center Management: Lessons Learned from 25 Years of Decentralized Management* (2002), Strauss and Curry report on their extensive conversations with senior leaders at the University of Pennsylvania and the University of Southern California after their systems had been in place for many years. Prominent among the lessons:

- Revenue incentives generally work—for entrepreneurs; they do not necessarily create entrepreneurs out of pie dividers; and related,

- RCM challenges traditional modes of academic leadership, requiring levels of management and financial prowess among provosts and deans not typically found or culturally developed in highly centralized systems; leadership changes are often required to make RCM successful.

- Allocations of university revenues (subventions in their terms) to schools can ossify into entitlements unless continually reviewed and altered or renewed—presidents and provosts need to own and continue to redirect a significant portion of university revenues to retain the ability to steer the university toward broad or common objectives;

- Talk about allocation rules and incentives can consume all the time available unless countered by serious talk about academic priorities and directions; and

- The fewer and simpler the rules, the more time for meaningful conversation.

Priest, *et al*, (2002) provide several perspectives, from examining RCM in the theoretical context of models of perfect and imperfect competition, to individuals' personal evaluations of how variations of RCM have been working in their particular university settings. We note John Douglas Wilson's chapter, *The Efficiency of Responsibility Center Management within State Universities,* where RCM is examined from multiple models of economic competition. Primarily in the context of imperfect competition, Wilson considers the impacts on decisions and outcomes of: student heterogeneity (differences in ability and preferences); externalities (for example, high-ability students lower the costs of attracting other students to an academic department, low-ability students raise them); reputation and free-riding (the ways in which weak departments can benefit from stronger, improving departments, and vice versa); asymmetric units (very large schools vs. small ones), and the like.

Finding several ways in which relatively "pure" RCM leads to sub-optimal decisions, Wilson then compares his analysis of RCM with relatively "pure" centralized decision systems. He notes that the distance from the point of action of the deciders makes them susceptible to lobbying efforts of the units—and appears to conclude that a regulated RCM approach may represent the right balance. In particular, he notes that the allocation of central base funding to periodically adjust for differential unit credit hour costs can obviate the problems that arise from simple tuition revenue allocation rules. He discusses other interesting interventions as well. He concludes with a point not often noted in other papers: How much discretion can be devolved or retained necessarily involves an investigation of political processes that operate on a campus.

We also note as worthy of further reading the chapter in Priest, et al, (2002) by Kenneth R.R. Gros Lewis and Maynard Thompson, in which they report and expand upon internal reviews in 1995-96 and 1999-2000 of RCM at Indiana University. They conclude "the case study for RCM is positive," with careful appraisals of the pros and cons along the way. The chapter, *Activity-Based Budgeting at the University of Michigan,* by Paul Courant and Marilyn Knepp, in which they chronicle the migration from RCM to Value-Centered Management (VCM) to the current Activity-Based Budgeting, describes the analyses and forces within University of Michigan that shaped the evolution of their approach to budgeting. They provide a particularly lively account of the University of Michigan's debate about whether to allocate tuition revenues on a credit-hour or numbers-of-majors basis.

Moving forward in time, we cite a paper by Cantor and Courant (2003). Writing from the perspective of the provost's office at the University of Michigan, they approach the tension between what they call "bottom line budgeting," a more general term for University of Michigan's variation of RCM called Value Centered Management (VCM), and public goods. They argue persuasively for the University of Michigan's mixed or hybrid model as a means both of preserving the entrepreneurship of departments and schools in the development of resources, and preserving the administration's ability to invest in public goods that would not be priorities from parochial perspectives. Among public goods (the commons), they note preservation of one's culture and history, even as one invests in untried innovations; the promotion of diversity and campus community engagement; the support of cultural institutions on campus; the exploration of intrinsically valuable but non-profitable disciplines; and the forging of interdisciplinary alliances. They do not argue that local entrepreneurship and support for public goods are mutually exclusive. Rather, they argue for getting the balance right between local and central roles and responsibilities and their respective shares of overall revenues.

The next notable source is James C. Hearn et al, *Incentives for Managed Growth: A Case Study of Incentives-Based Planning and Management in a Large Public University* (2007). In this paper, the authors extensively and carefully review the literature on incentive-based budget systems and provide a case study of the University of Minnesota's program, Incentives for Managed Growth (IMG). They chronicle the shift away from centralized incremental budgeting methods toward a program-performance emphasis, which couples local units' academic decisions with the direct financial consequences to the unit, and document the pros and cons of incentive-based budgeting as these evolve from theories as well as a rich trove of anecdotal data. They observe that on many campuses disagreements over the merits of incentive-based budgeting are ongoing, and often heated. But then they offer this gem: "... although the hortatory, critical and conceptual literature is ripe with cautions about the potential dangers of IBBS [incentive-based budget system] approaches to cooperation and collegiality on campus, two recent analyses (Gros Lewis & Thompson, 2002; Lang, 2001) present data suggesting that intra-unit efforts may actually be facilitated by IBBS approaches.... Clearly this arena is in need of more such evidence, and more of the 'Aha!' moments that only empirical research can deliver. The ratio of rhetoric to actual findings on the performance of IBBS is too high."

The authors then make a "modest attempt" to address this problem with their case study of IBBS at the University of Minnesota in the late 1990s. The authors develop a quantitative research methodology, and then measure results and follow up by interviewing a sample of deans. The results of their approach are presented in an evolutionary manner. The authors note that the IBBS system, no matter how aggressive, may not radically change budgetary outcomes or knowledge, and that the ultimate effects of IBBS in efficiency and effectiveness are [to that point] unclear. They go on to say that "practitioners and analysts should question some of the conventional wisdom regarding the likely effects of IBBS.... At the University of Minnesota, there were several surprises, and some early worries appear to have been unwarranted. ...evidence for assumed outcomes should always be pursued." A surprise finding from a preceding study (Kallsen, et al, 2001), for example, was that the two units with the largest growth in credit-hour generation were also those units that allowed their students to take the most courses outside their home unit. "These colleges have attempted to grow the enrollment pie, instead of dividing it, and have been the two most financially successful colleges under RCM practices."

In sum, Hearn, et al, state "the evidence reported here suggests that IBBS, when well integrated with a responsive, participatory planning system can contribute to institutional efficiency and productivity."

We move on now to Indiana University's internal RCM evaluations. Since Gros Lewis's and Thompson's 2000 review of RCM at Indiana, the university has undertaken two additional reviews. The most recent was in 2011 (which takes Indiana University's Bloomington campus across the 20-year mark with RCM). The review focuses on three items of interest: how the model is working during budget retrenchment, how the 2005 model changes have been accepted, and how the model impacts interdisciplinary activity. With respect to the first question, deans suggested that budget retrenchment has led to greater centralization, threatening the principles of RCM as a budgetary system.

They did, however, affirm the 2005 decision to increase the size of the provost's fund. Thus, it appears the deans felt it was important to maintain RCM in the retrenchment, and they did not show interest in abandoning their

RCM principles and attendant system. The deans also asked for increased transparency into the allocations from the provost's fund, and they noted that the efforts made in 2005 to simplify indirect cost pools and their allocations were received very positively. Deans stated that the move to simplicity "was a move in the right direction, a major improvement".

The third question about interdisciplinary activity is especially germane since it addresses a common and facile criticism of RCM. Members of Indiana's RCM Review Committee report that they extensively explored the claim that RCM adversely impacts interdisciplinary activity, and found that real barriers to interdisciplinary cooperation did indeed exist, though the committee did not find any evidence that RCM was itself the source. The committee even stated the opposite: that "RCM served to make transparent the actual costs and financial trade-offs involved in cross-RCM activity, and as a result, fostered healthy conversations about the underlying substantive merits of interdisciplinary proposals".

We cite finally a report commissioned by the University of California, Berkeley, and developed by the Hanover Research Council in 2008. The study added to existing literature by exploring the extent at which RCM models were devolved beyond the school/college level to departments. The report documents that 60% of the institutions studied carried RCM principles and structures to the school/college level while the rest had devolved revenues all the way to departments. The study also attempted to tackle a traditional RCM criticism, noting that "it is certainly not inevitable that RCM will result in declines in academic quality". The study went on to outline a handful of strategies to address the risk that RCM will create a culture that is overly focused on financials. Among the strategies noted are the earmarking of funds for collaborative programs (prioritizing subvention in our terms), the need for a one-year lag in the formula for revenue allocation to address volatility (the stable environments maxim we posited in 2002 and again in this edition), and the need to have a material subvention fund to maintain flexibility (one of the problems we address as "failing to hold the center" in 2002).

As we noted at the beginning of this chapter, our bibliography is long relative to our review. Interested readers can find a lot more food for thought by taking deeper dives into any one of the listed references.

CHAPTER FIVE

A Close-Up Look at Nine RCM Universities:
Case Studies from Conception to Maturity

We continue our assessment of how RCM is working
with relatively in-depth looks at nine universities.

With centralized budgeting, provosts, CFOs,
and CAOs dispense massive numbers of small
favors—such as faculty slots, secretarial positions,
information system resources, and physical space—
through an often unknown "black box" process.
Authority is local (residing in departments, labs, and
schools), responsibility is central, and the two are out
of balance, which creates a wide range of problems.

RCM promises a better way, one in which people
receive the information that connects all of the
budget's moving parts. RCM is not perfect, however,
nor does it work at every institution. Both Miami
and South Carolina, for example, implemented RCM
only to quickly retreat from it: Miami some 30 years
ago as the provost's forgiveness of deficits in some
schools precluded access to surpluses in others;
South Carolina more recently because precipitous
declines in state appropriation, the only source of
subvention, precluded redistribution of resources
to shore up priority programs. Some institutions,
including UCLA, have made a run at RCM but stopped
short of unleashing its inherent incentives and
responsibilities. A few others, including Vanderbilt
and USC, have taken steps to partially re-centralize
their approaches to financial management.

Of the many institutions that are adopting or have adopted an RCM model, this chapter briefly profiles nine of them. The information for these case studies came from publicly available data and reports, institutional presentations, stakeholder interviews, and direct implementation involvement, in addition to first-hand interaction. Each yields valuable lessons.

The nine case studies are arranged to reflect the lifecycle of RCM. The first, for example, focuses on how to begin an RCM conversation, while the second concentrates on RCM in its first "live" year. The third discusses how administrative services can become a primary driver of RCM development, and the fourth describes RCM development in the context of complex state rules governing revenues. The last five focus on changes to, and the vitality of, mature RCM universities.

The cases are:

1. All About Funds Flows—University of Kentucky

2. Taking Time to Build Consensus—Medical University of South Carolina

3. Optimization Through Customer Service—Ohio University

4. Developing RCM in the Context of Complex State Rules, Implementation Timing and the Times—Texas Tech University

5. Ongoing Evaluation—Indiana University

6. Still in Love After 35 Years—University of Pennsylvania

7. Migration Toward the Center—University of Southern California

8. Migration Toward Efficient Taxation—University of Michigan

9. Pullback From ETOB—Vanderbilt University

Note: This book defines RCM as any budget model that devolves revenues, allocates costs, and collects central resources for redistribution. Many practitioners and policymakers including some of the institutions profiled below use different terms, often classifying their models as incentive-based, activity-based, or hybrid.

◆ CASE STUDY 1:
ALL ABOUT FUNDS FLOWS
UNIVERSITY OF KENTUCKY

The University of Kentucky (UK), the state's flagship institution, has 16 colleges and enrolls more than 28,000 students. In fiscal year 2012, UK had operating expenses in excess of $2.3 billion.

In 2011, the University of Kentucky's president convened a committee to determine how the university could best serve its constituents in the next decade. Discussion centered on the higher education landscape, UK's mission and mandate, people, infrastructure, and resources. As part of its report, the review committee recommended putting in place a process to clarify strategic priorities and align resources accordingly. Historically, UK set its budgets at the prior year's base levels and adjusted for salaries, or reduced across the board to reflect cuts in state appropriations. It had limited provisions to facilitate strategic objectives.

To address the committee's recommendation, the president formed the Financial Systems Accountability Committee (FSAC). Chaired by the dean of the college of pharmacy, the committee included three other deans and a broad spectrum of university stakeholders representing faculty, staff, and administrators. The FSAC was charged with developing a set of guiding principles and new budget model framework, which together would address how to align UK's future strategic investments with its mission; provide incentives to the colleges; and articulate stakeholders' roles, responsibilities, and authority. The committee was free to design whatever model would best serve the institution.

The FSAC agreed upon five foundational principles to guide development of the Kentucky model. One noted, "The university should ensure the alignment of authority for financial management decisions and responsibility for the outcomes of those decisions, and determine the right balance between centralization and decentralization ..." Another principle stated, "The budget should support a culture that responsibly rewards performance, collaboration, and entrepreneurship."

Guided by the principles, the FSAC commissioned development of a current budget "funds flow" to exhibit all sources of revenues and their pathways through the university to their ultimate destinations. The committee's observations included the following:

- In many cases, the allocation of resources did not align with the selected principles. For example, the pooling and subsequent allocation of tuition and appropriation revenues did not promote a shared understanding of enrollment dynamics and any relationship to expense budgets.

- Complex rules regarding the allocation of indirect cost recovery (F&A) clouded budgetary transparency. In particular, the rules did not connect indirect cost recoveries (F&A) and the costs that generated them (facilities, general administration, and departmental administration).

- Different rules governed revenue ownership and thus entrepreneurship, leading to misallocation of focus and unintended consequences. For example, units received proportional revenue growth if they increased student fees, but not necessarily if they grew enrollment; this created an incentive to augment student fees independent of tuition hikes, which were decided by central administration. As a result, units might see the revenues once, while student wallets would be opened twice.

Exhibit A illustrates the flow as identified by the FSAC; it shows how complexities and confusion can accrue over time.

The misalignment of the funds flow with the guiding principles provided a case for change. Above all, the FSAC wanted the new model to reflect that the colleges and their faculty members were the primary drivers of revenues. The new model also needed to place the major academic units at the core of a revised funds flow.

Exhibit B provides the diagram that accomplished the FSAC's recommendations. Compared to Exhibit A, it is a model of transparency.

Using the new funds flow diagram as a foundation, the committee recommended that the university:

- Develop a simulation model to test specific allocation rules.
- Engage additional campus stakeholders in the effort.
- Develop a model for implementation in fiscal year 2014.

Lesson learned: You need to know what's so to determine what's next, to paraphrase an observation by Warren Bennis. A funds-flow model of the institution's current state can provide deep insights into budgeting structures and misalignments, and thus form the basis for change.

EXHIBIT A
UNIVERSITY OF KENTUCKY FUNDS FLOW
(PRE-FSA COMMITTEE RECOMMENDATIONS)

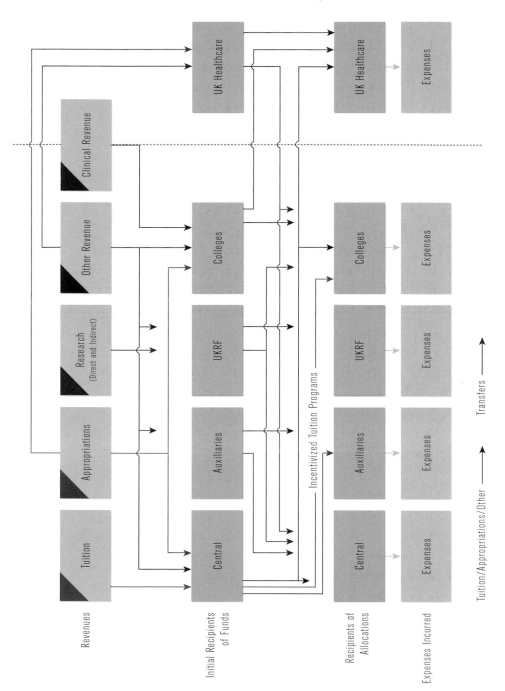

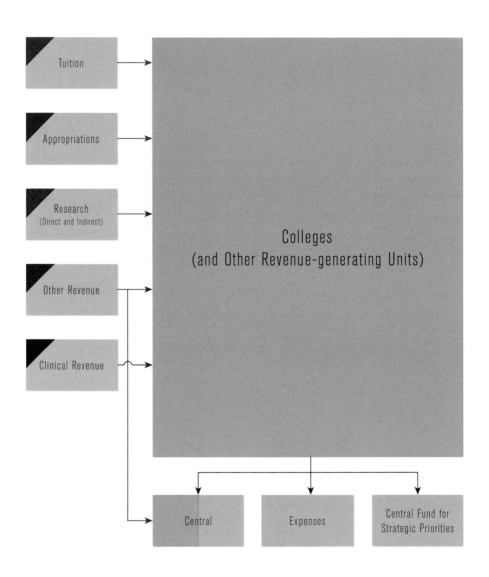

◆ CASE STUDY 2:
TAKING TIME TO BUILD CONSENSUS
MEDICAL UNIVERSITY OF SOUTH CAROLINA

Founded in 1824, the Medical University of South Carolina (MUSC) is recognized as the first medical college in the South. It has six colleges, almost 5,000 faculty and staff members, and more than 2,500 students. MUSC's 2012 fiscal year operating expenses exceeded $590 million (excluding the hospital and other component units).

The Medical University of South Carolina began evaluating its institutional funds flows in 2004 under the direction of the vice president for administration and finance with the advent of the Funds Flow Advisory Committee. Although the committee produced a "Funds Flow Manual," and while the efforts led to several key changes over the ensuing five years, the hoped-for transformation was not achieved —all for want of consensus. Here's how one associate dean summarized the university's challenge: "I have been here a long time, and change is desirable, but there are conflicts. Change is a hard pill to swallow."

MUSC's focus on change intensified in 2009. In the midst of unprecedented reductions in state support, limitations on tuition pricing, and systemic changes in the nation's approach to healthcare, MUSC established the Funds Allocations for Educational Activities Task Force to examine the sources and allocations of all funds across its schools and programs. In its 2009 report, the task force described an excessively complex system in which the original rationales governing budgets were either unknown or no longer applicable. The decades-old budget model was not well suited to decision making in the complex and volatile environment of the 21st century. In addition, many revenue sources were no longer coupled with the costs that gave rise to them.

Flowing from this critique, the task force made four recommendations:

• Adopt a budgetary philosophy from which principles and practices flow.

• Implement the new philosophy, and establish a hold-harmless transition period.

• Create a Budgetary Affairs Advisory Committee.

• Implement accountability for mission-based funding through an established review process.

The original task force comprised 19 members, including four of the institution's six deans, and the findings and recommendations appeared unanimous. Immediate progress was delayed, however, as MUSC grappled with precipitous reductions in state appropriations and executive turnover— including the departure of the provost, dean of medicine, and an associate dean for finance and administration.

In 2009 the new vice president for academic affairs and provost, along with the vice president for administration and finance, charged a Funds Flow Steering Committee with picking up where the task force had stopped. The steering committee began meeting weekly in 2010. Its first report spent 38 pages just explaining the institution's funds flows. Further, the report documented three different revenue-sharing approaches, eight university fees, and 44 college fees. From simple beginnings to create revenue incentives, the university had evolved into unmanageable budgetary complexity. One could no longer understand the consequences of specific actions.

The steering committee affirmed many of the earlier task force's findings and developed guidelines for a new approach to institutional resource management. Its members unanimously adopted six key characteristics of a new approach:

1. Transparency and integrity

2. Responsibility commensurate with authority

3. Flexible, scalable, translatable

4. Balance between central and local budget authority

5. Incentive driven

6. Enables forecasting and strategic planning

Distilling these six characteristics into a philosophy, the committee members agreed to move expeditiously to develop and implement a new model. They set a target of July 2011, leaving only eight months to develop a model with full consensus.

The desire for a transparent, incentive-driven approach naturally led to formulations and testing of RCM-like models. After documenting the pros and cons of various approaches, the steering committee presented its business case for a new budgeting model during a leadership retreat in February 2011. The case stated that the previous 14 weeks had entailed more than 100 meetings and discussions with more than 35 stakeholders.

Consensus emerged that MUSC's approach to resource management and allocation needed to change so it would enable more distributed and agile responses to changes in state support and to further new academic ambitions. In addition to outlining consensus on the six desired characteristics, the case noted that the model should allocate revenues to seven responsibility centers, and allocate 41 indirect costs pools using eight unique drivers. The case also outlined consensus on the need for a strategic investment fund.

Still undecided at the time were the distribution algorithms for tuition dollars and state appropriations. A subsequent retreat was held in late March to finalize the revenue allocations and preview the procedures for generating and redistributing indirect revenues. Between retreats, scores of analyses were conducted and many documents distributed to the leadership team to field queries and guide discussions. In May 2011, the proposed model—populated with multiple years of data—was presented at a third pre-implementation retreat. The provost and vice president for administration and finance gave a full accounting of indirect revenues, outlining expenses from the strategic initiative fund, as well illustrating the anticipated redistribution of indirect revenue. Final consensus was reached during this retreat, with each of the members of the leadership team pledging his or her support of the new model with a signature and a festive toast.

Lesson learned: Extensive stakeholder involvement, openness to any and all questions, and leadership persistence—these are necessary conditions for moving an institution from identifying a problem (the funds flow convolution), to building consensus that a problem exists, to characterizing the nature of an ideal solution, to developing and creating ownership of that solution. This case study also emphasizes the importance of the relationship between the provost and the vice president for administration and finance. These leaders should be on the same page and working in concert to build consensus. MUSC continues to hold periodic leadership retreats to deepen mutual understanding of its new ways of developing and deploying resources.

◆ CASE STUDY 3:
OPTIMIZATION THROUGH CUSTOMER SERVICE
OHIO UNIVERSITY

Ohio University (OU) was founded in 1804 as one of the very first public universities in the nation, and Ohio now has approximately 35,000 students, 11 colleges, five regional campuses, and two educational centers. For fiscal year 2012, OU had operating expenses of approximately $594 million.

The responsibility center management (RCM) efforts at Ohio University (OU), Athens, included several traditional elements. OU made use of a steering committee to develop a funds flow analysis, and applied principles to design incentives. However, the university's approach also incorporated a focus on institutional service levels that is all too often absent from most RCM implementations. In fact, the institution integrated its RCM efforts into the Ohio Service Alignment Initiative.

Although a resources implementation team had suggested adopting an RCM system, the recommendation languished for the next few years as leadership changes and effects of the 2008 recession intervened. Progress resumed in 2010 after the arrivals of a new provost and vice president for finance and administration. The latter recognized that implementation success often depends upon the efficiency and effectiveness of the central services allocated to the schools. Acknowledging that sub-par services could to lead to excess wrangling over allocation rules—and to expensive redundancy if centers grew their own local administrative units—OU launched its Ohio Service Alignment Initiative (OSAI).

The initiative began where the resources implementation team had left off, with the evaluation of OU's draft RCM model. The OSAI's model diagnostic evaluated the structure, rules, and incentives inherent in the model, which resulted in several modifications. In addition, the OSAI Committee embarked on a capacity analysis to assess OU's readiness for change. Focusing on elements of change management, project management, and information technology, the committee uncovered a number of major concerns:

- Suboptimal administrative and support-unit service levels.

- Suboptimal transparency with respect to administrative and support budgets.

- Absence of trust between colleges and the central administration.

- Limited confidence regarding the administration's technical capabilities and access to data.

OU outlined a three-year program to transition to RCM and address each concern along the way. For RCM to be successful, for example, administrative support units needed clear definitions of the services provided, responsiveness to customer needs, efficient delivery of services, and accountability for providing services at agreed-upon levels and prices. Over 16 weeks, current state assessments, desired future states, and the gaps in between were developed for three key areas: Finance, HR, and IT. Some 59 "gap-closing" recommendations came forward.

Armed with the OSAI Committee recommendations, OU decided that the success of RCM hinged on three equally important efforts:

1. Enhancing customer service levels.

2. Building institutional capacity.

3. Building college-level capacity.

To move forward expeditiously, OU developed a program management office to coordinate, manage, and integrate the implementation of the service assessment recommendations in a structured and methodical way. Exhibit C shows the committees and their reporting relationships:

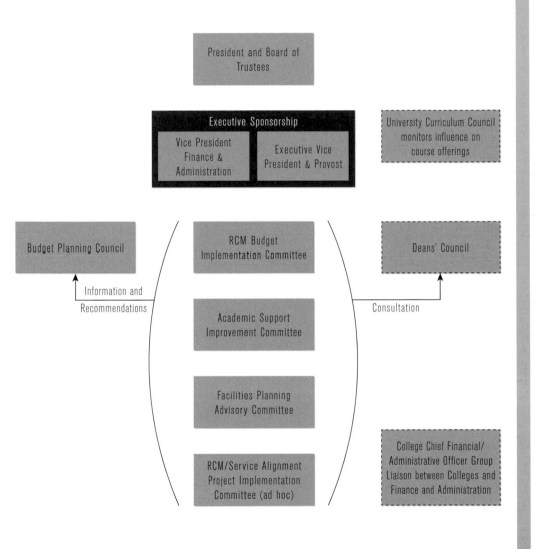

- The Budget Planning Council, an existing committee, was charged with linking the activities of the RCM Budget Implementation Committee with the Service Alignment Project Implementation Committee. The Budget Planning Council also reviews and recommends budget allocations to the executive vice president/provost and the vice president of finance and administration.
- The University Curriculum Council maintains its historical focus on curriculum but also monitors the impact RCM has on course offerings.
- The Facilities Planning Advisory Committee maintains its historical charge of overseeing deferred maintenance and space management.
- The RCM Budget Implementation Committee includes the provost, vice president for finance and administration, and three deans. It will refine and implement the RCM model and oversee the eventual five-year review process.
- The Academic Support Improvement Committee will review funding requests from cost centers; review cost center performance, based on service level agreements and KPIs; and direct cost center improvement efforts.

Lesson learned: Steven Covey's "1ˢᵗ principle" comes to mind: Start with the end in mind. With agreement about the desire for a common RCM structure at OU, the move to involve the often-overlooked administrative component of RCM at the outset is proving effective as the university continues rolling out its RCM initiative. Even mature RCM systems can benefit from service-level agreements and a structured review of administrative services.

◆ CASE STUDY 4:
  CONFRONTING COMPLEX STATE RULES
  TEXAS TECH UNIVERSITY

Texas Tech University (TTU) comprises 11 colleges and enrolls more than 31,000 students. In fiscal year 2012, TTU had operating expenses in excess of $652 million.

In 2009, a task force representing all constituencies—and including two regents—issued an enthusiastic recommendation for Texas Tech University to embrace RCM. Over the next two years, with the president's enthusiastic support, the task force provided policy oversight for implementation of an RCM model tailored to TTU's historic role and future ambitions to be formally recognized as a national research university.

Compared to other RCM installations at both public and private universities, TTU presented some significant challenges. On the positive side, TTU had a new, visionary strategic plan for achieving recognition by the state coordinating board as a national research university. The strategic plan depended upon RCM to facilitate development of new and reallocated resources to implement the highest priority objectives.

The challenges to implementing RCM ranged from limits in the university's historical business practices to the coordinating board's statewide higher education policies. For example, board policies included formula funding, purpose restrictions on appropriations and student fees, and the state practice of appropriating additional funds to cover most fringe benefits for employees paid from state funds. Because the state and/or coordinating board impose the purpose restrictions, these funds remained unrestricted in a formal accounting sense, but the purpose restrictions complicated the management as well as the accounting. Moreover, the ability to carry forward unrestricted fund balances to the second year of the biennium, enabled by state biennium budgeting, complicated application of some RCM practices developed for universities where unrestricted funds are collapsed into a single fund balance each year.

Historically, TTU did not have program budgets for many educational and support activities. Rather, individual elements of salary and program expense were budgeted in the financial system by area at prior-year levels, with little regard for revenue and little enforceable provision to underwrite strategic objectives. RCM's greater responsiveness to revenue and strategic objectives proved challenging to many people unaccustomed to thinking in those terms.

In Texas, formula funding determines the operations support appropriation for each state university by weighting credits taught in the various disciplines and student levels by the average cost of producing those credits across the system. This is a blessing for institutions with increasing enrollments, particularly in science, technology, and graduate programs that carry larger weights.

Yet, while TTU's appropriation is weighted appropriately relative to other institutions, it does not necessarily reflect the absolute cost of education per weighted student credit hour (WSCH) at TTU, nor does it reflect what the cost should be for the quality level to which TTU aspires. Also, because the WSCH is determined for a counting year preceding the biennium, the appropriation lags the actual enrollment. These total institution features of formula funding are exacerbated when RCM employs formula funding to distribute the operations support appropriation to individual colleges where the enrollment may be changing even more rapidly than for the institution as a whole.

Given the public and political nature of tuition rates and increases, TTU has responded with myriad student fees. The students must approve many of the fees, all of which are required (and audited) to be spent only for the approved purpose(s). TTU charges academic fees for laboratory, information technology, library, advising, law school, and cultural activities. The student-related fees include international education, medical services, student recreation, student services, student union, university ID, student transportation, student athletic, student business services, application, and energy. The incidental fees apply to diploma, education abroad, reinstatement, and more.

Under RCM, the proceeds from all fees are credited to the appropriate RCM centers as fees revenue to support the justifying underlying services (allocated costs). Tracking the application of these individual fees in RCM to ensure their purpose restrictions are met would be a herculean (and confusing) task. Accordingly, TTU chose simple RCM allocation algorithms and used the underlying financial system accounts to demonstrate that fee restrictions were satisfied.

RCM makes clear that fees contribute to the total price of a TTU education. Accordingly, it would be important to establish uniform approval processes. These would ensure that explicit trade-offs are made between fee dollars directed to academic, administrative, student service, and auxiliary enterprise purposes, with similar rigor employed to deciding how to divide other unrestricted funds.

Finally, Texas funds a special Employee Benefits Appropriation to pay a portion of the costs of employee benefits for personnel whose salaries are paid from specific items of the state appropriations that permit funding salaries. Rather than determining whether individual state-funded salaries are paid from one of these permissible appropriations, TTU has planned budgets using an approximation that salaries paid from any state funds will have 77% (in FY2010) of their benefits covered. This approximation is reconciled to the actual percentage as a part of year-end audit. This same approach would be employed in TTU's RCM budget planning.

Despite these challenges, the implementation of RCM appeared to go well. Consistent pro forma RCM ASIF (as if RCM had been in place) models were developed for the actual financial results of FY2009 and FY2010, and a corresponding model was developed from the FY2011 budget. Concurrently, extensive educational materials were developed and individual meetings held with the academic deans, resource center directors, vice presidents of the administrative service centers, vice presidents, faculty senate, and the faculty and staff of each center. The meetings focused on the prospective impact of RCM on individual centers and their ways of doing business.

In the spring of 2011, this preparation culminated with the projection of individual center budgets in RCM format for FY2012. These projected budgets were reviewed with the TTU president, provost, and CFO for consistency and to set initial values for the center indirect revenues (subventions), reflecting both historical practices and new strategic priorities. Then the academic deans, resource center directors, and administrative vice presidents were asked to review and comment upon the resulting budgets before finalization.

In June 2011, TTU's version of RCM was sufficiently specified and simulated that all centers could develop their fiscal 2012 budget proposals in the new context. When confronted with the comprehensive change in approach and increasing uncertainties in public funding, however, TTU's administration decided that a full-blown implementation was too big a risk. The university announced that RCM would be scaled back and introduced gradually over the next few years. The financial planning focus would be narrowed to dealing with the public funding issue in the known context of business as usual.

Lesson learned: The proliferation of fees in state-funded systems often disables focus on how to aggregate and amass sufficient resources to fund strategic needs. TTU developed the big revenue picture while accounting for fee-related expenses to ensure compliance with restrictions behind the scenes. Essentially, RCM is a version of managerial accounting, working on top of the basic chart of accounts (which enables standard financial reporting). Implementation can be affected by timing and the times.

◆ CASE STUDY 5:
ONGOING EVALUATION
INDIANA UNIVERSITY-BLOOMINGTON

Indiana University enrolls more than 100,000 students, with approximately 40,000 of them on its Bloomington campus. Fiscal 2012 operating expenses exceed $2.6 billion. Indiana University–Bloomington (IUB) has 13 schools and colleges.

Indiana University–Bloomington, the first public research university to implement RCM (in 1990), has become a stalwart in the world of decentralized budgeting. From the start, the university considered RCM a dynamic system that would benefit from planned periodic reviews. IUB's reviews were designed to capture the perceptions and opinions of RCM stakeholders, develop an understanding of how RCM was impacting the institution, and outline necessary changes to the model to address internal and external variables.

The committee that conducted the first review in 1996 first identified and met with people and constituencies who would broadly represent campus opinions and had insights into and experience with RCM. Committee members also actively solicited advice and opinions from faculty and others. Each interview, typically conducted by two committee members, followed a set list of issues to discuss. The cumulative results then formed the basis of the committee's recommendations. Review committees were appointed again in 2000, 2005, and 2011 with implementation of recommendations in the following fiscal years. In every case, the committee began its report with some variation of this statement: "Based on its findings, the committee recommends that the current version of RCM be maintained with modifications."

While consistently performed, methodical, and structured, IUB's reviews do not simply rubber stamp the current model. The 2005 RCM Review Committee, for example, outlined 15 dominant findings. Some were accolades ("RCM makes units aware of student interest and needs, and students have benefited from improved course availability") and others were critiques ("The chancellor does not have adequate resources to sustain and enhance quality and to fund the campus common good").

The review conducted in 2011 coincided with the 20-year anniversary of IUB's implementation of RCM. In its report, the review committee documented the evolution of IUB's model and noted some of the most significant changes:

- **RCM Priorities:** The 1996 RCM Review Committee noted that the campus academic administration needed central resources, and a provost's fund was developed. The 2000 and 2005 committees both increased the size of this fund. The 2000 committee also recommended using provost's funds to foster inter-unit cooperation and simplifying the cost assessment system for non-instructional units. In 2005 the committee prioritized the need for predictability over accuracy in attributing costs.

- **Undergraduate Tuition:** Over the years, tuition allocations went full circle in two instances. Initially undergraduate tuition was allocated without regard to student residency; this changed with the 1996 review and changed back in 2003. In a similar fashion, the lag-time associated with student credit hour counts for the allocation of tuition changed in 1997 to a two-year lag, before reverting to a one-year lag in 2002.

- **Indirect Cost Recoveries:** In 1998, the model was amended to allow for 5% of cost recoveries to accrue to the vice president for research; previously, 100% were allocated to the school or college.

- **Cash Reserves:** The policy for governing the use of year-end cash reserves was amended in the 1990s to allow service units to keep 40% of balances. All academic units still retained 100%.

- **Cost Allocation:** The 2005 review recommended a revised assessment model that would provide simplicity for longer term planning. In 2010, additional transparency was introduced with the publication of assessment drivers for each of four support unit allocation factors. As published in the 2011 RCM Review Committee Report, schools and colleges were charged $13.46 per square foot occupied, $55.03 per credit hour taught, $14,257.31 per tenure-line faculty member, and $14,181.22 per non-tenure employee. The new system received a favorable response in the review and will continue as the method for assessing central costs.

- **Provost/Chancellor Funding:** The original implementation of RCM did not hold back funding for central allocations for the Chancellor or Provost. It was determined in the 1996 review, funding should be held back centrally to fund campus initiatives to enhance quality, foster inter-unit collaboration, and support the "common good". From 1997 to 2001, an annual chancellor's tax was collected, equal to 1.5% of state appropriations. Starting in 2002, a 0.2% expense tax was added for the schools and colleges and a 0.5% expense tax was added to the support units. Finally, in 2007 a one-time $10 million president's tax was collected across IU's campuses.

Lesson learned: By formalizing organizational learning as a process, IU has set a standard for other RCM institutions to follow. By leaving the RCM system essentially alone for five years, IU allows enough time to test the consequences of prior adaptations yet can respond to emerging problems in a predictable way. Each review creates priority recommendations with a timeline for addressing each issue. It is expected that all issues should be discussed and/or resolved prior to the next review. Although selective tampering with RCM at the margin can eventually lead to unintended complexity and unpredictable effects, Indiana's systematic and systemic assessments address each part and its relation to the whole.

◆ CASE STUDY 6:
STILL IN LOVE AFTER 35 YEARS
UNIVERSITY OF PENNSYLVANIA

The University of Pennsylvania (Penn) has almost 25,000 students across 12 schools. For fiscal year 2012, the university's operating expenses exceeded $5.8 billion.

Martin Meyerson, president of the University of Pennsylvania in the early 1970s, championed the development of responsibility center management (L.B. Salomon and J.C. Strauss, 1979), and it endures to this day without major changes.

By bringing marketplace incentives to higher education, Meyerson hoped to involve faculty and others in considering financial as well as academic issues when making trade-offs between competing claims for limited resources. Before, and to this day at many colleges and universities, faculty members considered only academic issues in budget and space allocation decision processes and then resisted administrative concerns for financial viability. Meyerson's insight into the effectiveness of decentralized management at both improving decisions and reducing administrator/faculty conflict proved prescient. Ultimately it helped create a climate where decisions could be made within the appropriate context, more rapidly, and with potentially greater collegiality.

As a result of Penn's transition, Penn deans report much greater attention to developing philanthropic and other external revenue by both their faculty and themselves than would be the case in more traditional management systems. The case of USC is instructive here as well. The schools of dentistry, pharmacy, and urban and regional planning literally built themselves on the enrollment and research revenue incentives of RCM. Other schools, like music, realized that, given unit costs, their further development could not come from enrollment but had to come from gifts and endowments. Coupling of marginal revenues with marginal costs led to appropriately different strategies among the schools.

Since Penn's implementation, many institutions have sought to mirror its success, yet two aspects of Penn's system remain unique:

- From the outset, student services have been funded directly through a specific student fee rather than through indirect cost pools allocated to the schools and paid for with their revenues.

- As the system matured, the university library was funded directly from subvention in recognition of its importance to the common good.

In the 1990s, Penn suffered what its budget director described as "ossification of subventions," as well as growth in administrative services that duplicated their central counterparts within the responsibility centers. In addition, many newcomers did not understand the principles behind or the structure of RCM. Solutions involved recognizing that subventions could be reduced in centers having excess local central administrations, relieving the apparent need for local services through renewed focus on the quality of central services. Penn did not change its rules; active management, using the tools already available, righted the balance.

Lesson learned: Active management is required; the intellectual case for RCM needs refreshing as seasoned players leave and new leaders arrive. Ideally, any institution adopting or using the model should retain or find a resident RCM "zealot" to explain and defend the system.

◆ CASE STUDY 7:
MIGRATION TOWARD THE CENTER
UNIVERSITY OF SOUTHERN CALIFORNIA

The University of Southern California (USC) has more than 38,000 students across 20 academic units. In fiscal year 2012, the university had operating expenses just shy of $3.2 billion.

Since RCM "went live" at the University of Southern California in 1982-83, the university's design for its revenue centers has changed over time. Here are the noteworthy changes:

- In 2002, frustrated with ongoing contention over the growth in administrative indirect costs, the university "guaranteed" these costs would not rise more than a modest pre-specified percent over time. By taking attention away from indirect costs through a simple guarantee, the university removed much of the incentive for deans to challenge service costs. The guarantee, however, did not obviate the need to increase indirect costs. Indeed, as pressures mounted to address classroom renovations and enhance campus security, USC adhered to its indirect cost pledge but introduced a new tuition revenue tax earmarked to fund emerging needs (thus, indirect costs became revenue earmarks). In recent years, the distorting effects of not systematically reallocating administrative costs in proportion to the appropriate drivers have led to a rebalancing of the true indirect costs and their allocations and some specific reviews of administrative centers. But questions remain about how or whether to allow indirect costs to be dynamically allocated in the future.

- USC retracted to the center its Ph.D. tuition revenues. Leaders viewed this as more optimally allocating the increasingly significant tuition remission benefits and as focusing more intently on the care and feeding of Ph.D. students across the university. In particular, a chronic concern was graduate students taking courses in another school that were paid for with the tuition remission benefit from their majoring school. (The University of Michigan addressed the same problem by allocating a larger portion of graduate tuition to the majoring school.)

- Over the years, USC's participation rate (tax) has declined from the original level of 20% to approximately 8%. The basic reason is straightforward: As individual schools decreased their needs for subvention, either through revenue growth or acquisition of major endowments, much less redistribution of revenues was needed to achieve balance across the schools. At one time, for example, USC's music school needed $3 million more than the participation it contributed to balance. Then the school received a major gift to endowment, which vastly reduced its need for subvention.

- Accrued balances in the USC "inter-center bank" are now retained in a provost's account—but in the schools' names. Rather than guarantee a percentage withdrawal each year, as in the original design, deans now must seek the provost's approval. Deficits are now covered from designated fund balances. This appears to introduce an asymmetry into budget performance incentives.

Taken together, these changes in the rules represent significant recentralization of authority and responsibility. In USC's original conceptualizations of RCM, deployment of subvention and quality measures provided central leverage.

Lesson learned: Changing contexts may require changes in the rules governing RCM. Leaders' own senses of central power and the relative importance of policy can lead to rebalancing of authority and responsibility. However, rigorous deployment of subventions and active negotiation of indirect costs and their allocations might have achieved the same ends. Introducing revenue earmarks beyond the participation tax to fund facilities and security-related costs adds complexity and contributes to a less efficient system. If there is a case for higher indirect costs, leadership needs to make it and increase allocations.

After that, therefore because of that? By way of history, we note that when USC implemented RCM in 1982, the institution had an endowment of nearly $200 million, an application pool of less than 10,000, an acceptance rate exceeding 60% (with yield less than 40%), entering SAT scores around 1000, and first-year student retention of 70+%. Thirty years later, the endowment has reached $3.5 billion, the application pool exceeds 40,000, the acceptance rate is 23% (with a yield of 50%), and first-year retention has climbed to 96%. Certainly, robust leadership teams have had an impact on the institution; the case is strong that USC's RCM model also helped strengthen the university's financial operations and position.

◆ CASE STUDY 8:
   MIGRATION TOWARD EFFICIENT TAXATION
   UNIVERSITY OF MICHIGAN

The University of Michigan (UM) has more than 42,000 students across 20 schools and colleges. In fiscal year 2012, the university's operating expenses exceeded $5.8 billion.

Since adopting its version of RCM in 1990, the University of Michigan has used several names for it: value-centered budgeting, activity-based budgeting, and simply university budget (UB). UM is a public institution and, like Indiana University, retained central ownership of the state appropriation as the major component of the subvention pool. It initially charged a participation tax of 2%—quite low at the time, given the heft of state money.

A material change occurred around 2000. Michigan pooled its central administration costs and allocated the sum according to a single driver—total direct expenses. Included in this overall expense tax was a new assessment to replace the original 2% revenue tax (participation).

The UB model leaves a fair amount of room for the president and provost to exercise their own judgment. Compared to other RCM models, UM's version appears to provide more central and discretionary funding. Indeed, under UM's model, the provost captures increases in state appropriations, an 11% tax on externally sponsored research, a 2% tax on auxiliary operations, a 21% tax on organized research units, and a 24% tax on schools and colleges. (The latter is a means of collecting pooled central administrative costs and funding a central discretionary pool.) In each case, the taxes are applied to expenses.

Michigan has calculated maintenance costs and metered utility costs per square foot for each building; all occupants of a given building pay the same rate. Further, a position in the provost's office is charged with serving as a broker of space. Knowing occupancy and space needs, the internal broker can prompt discussions about trading space. Although deans rarely swap space between schools, serious attempts to optimize space occur within schools. UM plans to charge its centers for renewal based on square footage occupied and to centralize the deployment of such funds. While the charge will be uniform over time, expenses will not be; the centers will benefit when their time for renovations comes.

Lesson learned: Simplifying the administrative services "tax code" and charging a direct expense tax to fund the subvention pool appear to be working. Both are testimony to the political benefits of parsimony and the economic benefits of efficient taxation.

◆ CASE STUDY 9:
PULLBACK FROM ETOB
VANDERBILT UNIVERSITY

Vanderbilt University enrolls 13,000 students and comprises 10 colleges and schools. It had more than $3.5 billion in operating expenses during the 2012 fiscal year.

Each Tub on its Own Bottom (ETOB) is an extreme form of decentralized management adopted by Vanderbilt in the early 1980s. It worked well for Vanderbilt until the 2008 recession made the ETOB system seem like an obstacle. Where collaboration was needed to deal with large changes, silo behavior seemed endemic. Where clear sight lines into the financial circumstances (revenues, expenses, balances) of the tubs were needed to assess the university's overall state in real time and work with units on financial solutions, central leadership could not access the needed information directly and had to rely on locally generated reports to get the whole picture. Where administrative economies of scale were needed to balance budgets without directly affecting academic programs, central leadership found multiple admissions and registrar offices (among other duplicative services) across the tubs.

In response, the chancellor carved out a focused chief financial officer position from the former, much broader administrative role and required business officers in the schools (tubs) to report to the new CFO. Vanderbilt also pulled back undergraduate tuition to central ownership, to be managed and allocated by the president and provost.

Lessons learned: Excessive decentralization can provide as many problems as excessive centralization. The changes at Vanderbilt, often considered an RCM institution but really not, moved the university back toward a balanced structure. The primary advantages expected as a consequence of the recentralization can be (and usually are) part of an RCM system that features robust financial and business intelligence.

Unlike an RCM system that retains material and appropriate central leverage, an ETOB system does so only when the center owns a huge unrestricted endowment. Vanderbilt responded to this ETOB problem by asserting 100% central ownership of a specific revenue stream: undergraduate tuition. In addition, an RCM system needs a robust central financial accounting system that all users understand and embrace, one capable of producing revenue and expense statements, at any level of the organization, virtually on demand. Thus, real-time assessment of financial performance and accountability substitute for tight controls. Lacking such real-time capability in tough times, Vanderbilt asserted control over the business officers in the tubs to gain more direct access.

CHAPTER SIX

How RCM is Working: Promises vs. Performance Updated

Moving from a central budgeting system to a distributed one like RCM entails a lot of work. Along the way, two valid questions arise: Is it worth the time, effort, and money to change? Will the performance be commensurate with its promise?

To help answer those questions, this chapter builds upon the two prior chapters, draws upon three decades of the authors' experiences with RCM as practitioners and consultants, and synthesizes discussions and interviews with some 40 RCM leaders and stakeholders across more than a dozen RCM institutions. As one might expect, the takeaways are mixed, with both success stories and failures. On balance, the positives outweigh the negatives, and amended approaches can address most, if not all, of the criticisms and challenges raised.

SIX PROMISES FULFILLED

Conversations with those whose institutions employ RCM yielded these general themes—all reinforcing and complementing our findings in 2002 and supported in the literature review and case studies:

1. **Leadership stakes are higher all around in RCM.** Stakeholders consistently reported that in an RCM environment, presidents, provosts, deans, and unit heads must lead academically and actively manage financially, not simply administer. Not all deans or administrators are up for this task. RCM is a call to action: to be entrepreneurial, to be explicit about local and central priorities, to maintain the right balance between authority and responsibility, to be transparent about decision making and centers' financial performance, and to maintain efficient and effective administrative services. Failure to rise to this call at any key position across the leadership spectrum undermines RCM's promise.

   To borrow from Warren Bennis's observation, you need strong leaders to do the right things; you need strong managers to do things right. The more durable RCM universities acknowledge that the leadership stakes have risen over time and they are benefiting from broader and more engaged leadership teams. At the same time, some institutional retreats from full RCM systems or implementation efforts can be traced to leadership discomfort with the "constructive tension," financial management expectations, and transparency inherent in RCM.

2. **RCM enhances commitment to long-term planning.** Stakeholders consistently reported that their RCM models enhance long-term focus at the school level. The most commonly cited reason is the existence of rules that unit leaders can trust and rely upon when considering, say, the creation of new academic programs. Also cited are specific policies, such as retention of surpluses to enable future years' start-ups or capital investments, and the way local responsibility for future facilities' financing costs requires balancing fundraising goals (equity capital) with debt. The goal is to ensure that future years' budgets can cover debt service—not to mention the allocated maintenance costs that new space brings.

3. **Enrollment incentives work.** Virtually all participants indicated that allocating enrollment revenues to centers improves their responsiveness to course needs and opportunities for enrollment growth. As one stakeholder noted, "Academic units appear to pay much better attention to course and program design in order to maximize their revenue return." While couched financially, "better attention to course and program design" is bound to provide benefits to students in both the quality and availability of core and major-specific courses. The case of Indiana University is exemplary here.

FIXING THE PIPELINE:
THE THREAT OF INTERNAL COMPETITION IMPROVES CORE COURSES

Aware of their enrollment-related revenues, the faculty of engineering at USC in the late 80s became alarmed at the rate highly qualified engineering freshmen were failing prerequisite physics courses. They asked, "Why are these bright students failing physics, and thus endangering future enrollments and numbers of majors in engineering, when they are doing well in calculus and introductory engineering courses?" After rather boldly sitting through physics lectures with freshman, engineering faculty concluded that the problem lay with the physics faculty rather than the students, and challenged their physics colleagues to improve their courses and pedagogy. Since many engineering faculty held Ph.D. degrees in physics, the very real threat to teach their own introductory physics courses led to reform in the physics department (whose dean did not want to lose large course revenues). This story exhibits a positive outcome from knowing the costs of one's actions and who bears them.

4. **Research incentives work.** When schools see explicitly their facilities and administration indirect costs, break them down between instruction and research, and then compare the latter with their indirect cost recoveries (F&A), they can compare costs incurred with costs recovered. And typically those costs exceed the reimbursements by wide margins. The questions then arise: Why? And how can we increase our recoveries? Some or all of the following are answers: The university has not been aggressive or successful at negotiating the indirect cost recovery (F&A) rate; there are no policies (or controls) on involuntary cost sharing on federal grants—faculty may be volunteering to accept indirect cost recovery (F&A) rates below the negotiated rate to appear more price competitive; or similarly there may be a large number of state or foundation grants which pay minimal overhead. Thus, RCM financial statements at the school level enable faculty member to understand that there are real and quantifiable costs associated with under-collection of indirect costs from grants. We have seen deans conferring with faculty members about reducing degrees of cost sharing and talking with sponsored research officers to urge more aggressive negotiating stances. This provides a counterweight to faculty arguments that the university should keep indirect cost recovery (F&A) rates low.

Also, when indirect cost recoveries (F&A) are allocated to schools that incur research-related indirect costs, a further incentive is allocating the departmental administration component of the rate further down the organization chart to departments and faculty members generating the research.

5. **Quality and strategic assessments are mediated by bottom lines.** Once RCM is in place and people have understood what lies behind relative subventions or indirect revenues (net or fully costed margins), assessments of quality and of strategic importance take on a new dimension, going from benefit analysis to benefit-at-what-cost analysis. Thus one might ask: Is school or program X worth the heavy investment of university resources relative to its quality and strategic priority? Does X have the opportunity to be more self-supporting? If so, why is it not? If it cannot be, is it nonetheless vital to our mission and strategy? We have seen such conversations become commonplace across the many RCM universities we have come in contact with.

6. **Reliance on data has increased data quality.** Stakeholders frequently commented on the importance of institutional data in developing and operating their RCM models, noting that new uses of data led to intense scrutiny of all data systems. The data RCM puts into play typically include credit hours and majors (and where they are produced or reside), space occupancy and costs to maintain different types of space, various headcounts and FTEs, the legitimacy of restrictions across gift and endowment funds, measures of performance across administrative service units, and new quality measures to compete with financial performance measures.

While no one wished to relive the process of reviewing and scrutinizing such data, the institutions emerged from this exercise with a much higher degree of confidence in their institutional data. Stakeholders reported that this increased confidence has resulted in greater effectiveness: Conversations focus on the interpretation and meaning of the data, not on their validity—as typically happened before RCM.

SIX MYTHS PUT TO REST

There are several myths about RCM that our surveys, interviews, and discussions and the literature have at least partially debunked. *Contrary to myth:*

1. **Interdisciplinary programs are not hampered by RCM; they are indeed growing.** In almost every instance, we learned that institutions have more interdisciplinary courses, degrees, and research programs than they did in the past decade. While acknowledging that creating these programs was not necessarily easy, some stakeholders confidently stated that RCM had not been a barrier to the interdisciplinary activity. Rather, they reported that collaboration is a "leadership issue" and that the programs were created simply "because it is the right thing to do"—perhaps because interdisciplinary initiatives are part of their strategic plan. The strategic use of subvention can also give rise to multidisciplinary programs. During the 1990s and early

2000s, for example, the University of Southern California (USC) set aside part of its subvention pool to underwrite innovative proposals crossing school (center) boundaries—almost taking a venture capital approach. Indiana University's periodic reviews of this issue (See Chapters 4 and 5) indicate that, in fact, the clear structure of RCM provides a useful financial foundation for working out the details for multi-disciplinary programs.

2. **RCM does not necessarily result in course hoarding or trade barriers.** Roughly one of every 10 stakeholders reported that the budget model resulted in course hoarding or stealing. The other nine stated that the budget model was not driving undesired or duplicative course offerings. Most commonly, stakeholders reported the existence of a "curriculum approval process" and "course monitoring by academic affairs," which revealed real or potential course-grabbing initiatives and led to corrective peer pressure. Several stakeholders even suggested that the budget model itself alleviated competition for courses, stating that the "formula for core undergraduate courses mitigates the issue" by sharing revenues appropriately between the center of instruction and the center of record. Especially noteworthy here is the University of Minnesota's experience (Chapter 4).

3. **Schools may deploy enrollment incentives inappropriately, but regulation intervenes.** A department, for example, might "dumb down" courses or ease grading standards to encourage enrollment of students from other departments and schools (who would bring along their tuition revenues). "Gut" courses are not a new phenomenon, nor did they arise only because of the financial incentives in RCM. But RCM can certainly exacerbate the problem by adding revenue to popularity. Leadership can and should intervene. Quality control should modulate venality. Or, strategic regulation, potentially involving broad curricular changes, should and can modulate laissez faire. Structured course offering and curriculum review processes can work well in this arena.

A COURSE CORRECTION:
REGULATION MODULATES UNBRIDLED LAISSEZ FAIRE

In the early 1980s, when RCM took root at the University of Southern California (USC), the provost recognized that letters, arts and sciences majors could benefit from access to courses in the extensive array of professional schools on campus. The provost encouraged development of general education offerings within such schools as business, law, gerontology, public administration, cinema, theatre, and the like. The professional school deans saw revenue opportunities in such courses and proceeded accordingly.

The early years of this initiative clearly benefited liberal arts and sciences majors—and the offering schools. But in time, and with a change in provosts, financial incentives began overpowering academic intent. Indeed, some professional schools focused too much on their general education offerings, at the expense of their professional programs. Moreover, the array of general education offerings made less and less curricular sense, even as revenues were being drained from the letters, arts and sciences college.

The thinking that ensued led to clearly reasoned and defined minors in USC's professional schools, which still had positive revenue incentives, and brought order to the increasingly chaotic general education offerings. Newly designed minors provided a form of regulation that worked.

4. **Local optimization can—but need not—damage the whole.** Individual centers can take actions in their local interest that may ultimately diminish the common good. The disorderly proliferation of general education courses is a case in point—and many others exist as well. For instance, deans may urge reductions in student services, library costs, or facilities' budgets, even when these costs are necessary to their students and not unreasonable within the context of their competitive markets. The deans' goal: to reduce the indirect costs allocated to their centers and free up revenues for direct program support. Senior leaders must speak up for properly funding those programs that benefit the whole more than any individual (center) part. This is yet another rationale for revenue taxes to ensure critical central leverage.

    Here's another example of how RCM's incentives work well but, if left unmanaged, can lead to distortion of academic intent. In the early 1990s, many large private universities experienced dramatic drops in yield, and hence in freshman enrollments, at the same time that financial aid budgets soared. When confronted with their own tuition revenue losses, several deans of individual schools at USC proposed reducing the quality threshold for admission (to increase revenues) rather than reducing expense budgets. The president simply said no. Recognizing that the entire university's academic reputation was at stake, the president demanded that quality thresholds be raised, even if it meant accepting a significantly reduced—but better qualified—freshman class. Counter to the deans, the president saw that reducing revenues and raising quality were necessary to raising quality and revenues in the future.

    While the transition was painful, USC's applicant pool, yields, and academic quality of entering freshmen skyrocketed within a very short time (see the USC case study in Chapter 5). Arguably, that would not have happened if each dean had optimized his or her revenues. In such circumstances, central leadership must exert corrective action through persuasion, direct order, or corrective subvention allocations (if available).

5. **Focus on the bottom line does not subvert academic quality.** Academic considerations retained their priority status at every institution we talked with or reviewed despite fears that RCM would result in a focus on financial performance rather than academic quality. Stakeholders simply said they "do not believe the issue is significant" and pointed to the time and effort spent on long-term goals and academic plans. Stakeholders typically provided some variation on the statement that "RCM is part of the decision-making process but does not drive academic decisions."

6. **The rich do not get rich at the expense of the poor.** The myth emanates from centralized budget processes where the provosts and CFOs own the revenue pie—and the budget game is maximizing one's share. While RCM stakeholders confirmed that "the rich got richer," it was because of entrepreneurial leadership or a school's business model, reputation, and/or market opportunities. The growth "did not happen at the expense of other centers"—an oft-repeated phrase. And remember: RCM institutions with a participation fee will have additional resources in the subvention pool to provide support to academically deserving but relatively poorer schools.

RCM thus appears more a positive- than a zero-sum game. Indeed, schools such as business, engineering, and medicine typically respond well to the pie-expanding incentives of RCM, while deans of law are often particularly persuasive with provosts. And it sometimes seems that deans of arts and sciences are preternaturally preoccupied with allocation rules. RCM is a game: Entrepreneurs will learn how to play and win by the rules, while others will try to play with the rules to win. In the final analysis, senior leaders have the authority to appoint school leaders who can be successful, and they have the responsibility to guide these leaders through both word and deed.

SIX PROMISES UNFULFILLED

Despite its promise, RCM still and all too commonly experiences shortfalls in several areas.

1. **Public information invites misinterpretation—but provides its own foundation for correction.** USC, Claremont Graduate University, and the University of Pennsylvania, among others, report intervention by trustees in the algorithms for allocating administrative costs and awarding subvention funds. Public information can cause other problems, such

as invidious and unfounded comparisons of relative subventions. When people do not understand that a significant component of subvention neutralizes the effects of pairing differential costs of education with common credit-hour prices, for example, they may claim that one center is being ripped off while another is receiving unearned alms. Comparing schools of business and music is a case in point. The claim is almost always wrong. Left alone, without explanation, numbers can mislead.

In the early 1990s, when UCLA began to generate RCM budget profiles, the dean of medicine proclaimed that the indirect cost recoveries (F&A) from his school's federal grants and contracts were supporting the school of letters and sciences, among others. But when medicine's indirect costs were added to direct expenses and the sum compared with medicine's revenues, there were no revenues left to support anyone else. Moreover, when UCLA calculated the impact of large undergraduate enrollments on its state allocations, letters and sciences did not look needy after all. In this case, good numbers enabled understanding of the internal economics and purged unfounded, unsubstantiated, and harmful claims.

Lore based on no or limited data is no better than misinterpretation of good data. Indeed, it's far worse, because too little or poor data provide no foundation for recourse.

2. **Transparency is still lacking.** Many universities reported that, despite publishing extensive budget reports and following open allocation rules, units perceived a lack of transparency in budgeting. This perception appears directly related to the complexity of the allocation rules and budget-related policy: The more complex the rules, the greater the perception that the published budget is not the real story. As one stakeholder observed, "Though budget information is published, many on our campus believe that there are hidden stories that have never been divulged which would expose who really gets what funding for what reasons."

It is sometimes said that transparency is inversely related to the amount of information available. It's hard to develop simple budget reports that convey just the right amount of digestible information, and even when such reports are distributed, they often need clear explanatory notes to be truly useful and understood. Still more important are senior leaders' communications about how their subvention decisions explicitly recognize relative costs of instruction and derive from university priorities. *The moral*: Being open with respect to budgets and underlying rationale is often viewed as being transparent; but transparency is in the eye of the beholder and is "real"—that is, believed in—only if materials are presented clearly in readily understandable ways.

3. **Debate persists about indirect cost allocation rules.** No university surveyed had completely put to rest arguments about, and continual rehashing of, indirect cost allocation rules. Issues range from minor "noise" at long-lived RCM universities to near disruptions at universities that are relatively recent to RCM. Senior leaders are too often lured into such zero-sum negotiations at the expense of the time needed to focus on academic initiatives. Again, the onus is on leadership to quell useless bickering and extract constructive balance among the issues that matter.

4. **Administrative service efficiency and effectiveness mostly remain elusive.** Many stakeholders reported ongoing complaints from academic units that they do not receive their "fair share" of central services, that services provided are not useful to them, or they could perform the services better themselves. Meanwhile, service units claim to be underfunded with respect to the demands placed on them. These complaints, common in centralized budgeting systems as well, appear both an unfortunate and a continuing reality. Here, the data prompt both the right questions and unfounded allegations. Lacking is leadership willing to demand that administrative units demonstrate the effectiveness and efficiency of their services. Institutions using structured processes to review and analyze administrative costs and services fare better than the rest. Good processes are needed alongside structured incentives.

5. **RCM does not appear to be the silver bullet for managing space.** Incentives for efficient use of space do not appear to be working well. At almost every institution queried, space utilization and renewal remain problematic. Stakeholders reported that, "Even when billed for space occupation, units fear that releasing under-utilized space may put them at risk for recovering space in the future." Few internal markets appear to exist for the trading of space for dollars. One positive consequence of cost allocations for space, however, is that stakeholders reported "intense and productive" focus on who pays for newly constructed space. We know of two universities where structured brokerage functions bring units seeking additional space together with surplus space "owners." These work very effectively—yet another instance where incentives, to work well, require leaders to intervene.

6. **RCM systems do not necessarily take care of themselves.** Indeed, they need to be managed and modified as circumstances warrant. Common forms of unmanaged degradation include:

   - One-off changes of the rules to appease noisy plaintiffs.
   - Incremental migration toward more allocation precision at the expense of overall understanding of how the system works.

- Allowing subventions to ossify and thus turn into de facto entitlements.
- Periodic abrogation of incentives and responsibilities, such as denying future uses of earned surpluses or forgiveness of deficit repayments.
- Retraction to the center of a major revenue stream.
- Introduction of new leaders into the system who believe in industrial policy more than market competition—and thus begin reversing revenue devolution to achieve more central power.

Institutions need to be mindful that a sequence of well-intended, one-off changes can have unanticipated systemic effects. It's worth thinking again about Indiana University's approach: five-year reviews that consider, simulate the consequences of, and potentially make systematic changes to its version of RCM. An attendant benefit is the periodic opportunity to educate newcomers about why RCM was developed in the first place (See Case Study 5 in Chapter 5).

TWO EMERGING TRENDS

In the RCM world, two trends appear to be taking shape:

1. **Decanal entrepreneurship is not enough.** Most writings about RCM focus on unleashing and expecting entrepreneurship among the deans. They speak much less, if at all, to the provost's and president's roles as entrepreneurs. With collaborative and interdisciplinary activities becoming increasingly important and with the emergence of new areas of science requiring relatively massive investments in facilities and infrastructure, executive entrepreneurship is critical. Some programs are simply too big and complex to be developed and funded in any one school.

   Provosts need to develop new sources of funding for the subvention pool to seed large joint ventures. Joint plans to fund major facilities are emerging, with presidents taking the lead in securing large gifts around which the deans involved can develop their fundraising goals and financing plans.

2. **The tax and subvention model may is changing.** Several RCM institutions are eliminating the participation/subvention convention altogether. At issue is the fact that participation is not viewed as legitimately owned by the university; rather it is considered a tax on the schools' revenues. Also, more often than not, tax rates of 20% or so are considered confiscatory even though most of the proceeds go back to the schools that "pay" the taxes as subventions to balance revenues with expenses. In place of the participation/subvention approach, some RCM models may move to

targeted bottom lines—fully costed margins or indirect revenues, both positive and negative—as the foci for budget deliberations. The university "owns" these margins instead of portions of revenues generated by the schools. Each unit's anticipated bottom line would be established through the budget process each year, and the goal of balancing to zero would be held at the institution level, not the center level.

The overlapping arcs of our personal management and consulting experiences, the interviews and conversations we have recorded with leaders of RCM universities, and the applicable literature and case studies indicate that the fulfilled promises of RCM, especially the revenue incentives and attendant financial understandings of a university's internal and external economies, far outweigh the unfulfilled ones. This is especially so when we already know the kinds of management actions necessary to address the latter. We are reinforced in this evaluation by the degree of persistence over time of RCM institutions, and the continuing rates of conversion across a variety of universities from centralized to more decentralized approaches—and only one recent reversion to centralized budgeting in the case of the University of South Carolina early in its implementation cycle. But perfection is ever elusive: As our cases show, there is continuing movement even among long-standing RCM universities along the centralized-decentralized spectrum.

CHAPTER SEVEN

RCM-Enabled Analyses

When surveyed by the EDUCAUSE Center for Applied Research, 84% of responding institutions believed that analytics were more important than they had been two years previously (*Analytics in Higher Education*, 2012). The same report noted that finance and budgeting were the second most common uses of analytics in higher education, coming right after enrollment management. The report, however, concluded that while "institutions are collecting more data than ever... most of these data are used to satisfy credentialing or reporting requirements rather than to address strategic questions." In other words, data and related analytics to support decision making remains underdeveloped.

RCM provides a basic foundation for analysis by answering several questions directly: What revenues do the schools earn? What is the cost of space occupied by a given school? What portion of the whole enterprise is consumed by central administrative costs? At the same time, RCM raises additional questions that beg for further analysis: Why does one school have a large negative net margin (indirect revenue), while another has a positive one? Is it the higher cost of instruction in the school? Under enrollment relative to faculty available? Low effective indirect cost recovery (F&A)? Or something else?

Here are a few examples of how RCM can answer those questions—and many more.

FUNDS-FLOW ANALYSIS:
UNDERSTANDING THE INTERNAL ECONOMY

Universities often portray their budgets (or related actuals in financial statements) in the form of pie charts. Typically, one pie shows revenues and another shows expenses, but no explicit relationship appears between the wedges of the two pies. Typical RCM formats make the missing connections. We refer to Table 3 in Chapter 3.

Let's consider a simple question asked about the same institution under different budgeting approaches: What is the resource commitment to the college of business? If the institution operates in a centralized incremental budget mode, you would look at the college's expense budget on Line 23, Column 3 of Table 3 and say, "The college of business *consumes* $19.7 million of the university's resources."

A much different answer emerges from an RCM perspective: Looking at Line 35, column 3, you would say, "The college of business *contributes* $6.7 million to support the rest of the university." The two answers—to the same question—reflect a $26.4 million difference. The RCM answer recognizes the revenues generated by the school and its total costs (including indirect costs), then calculates its (positive) fully costed margin of $6.7 million. Still more accurately, you might say, "The college of business produces revenues in excess of total costs of $6.7 million, thus exporting resources to fund other programs."

Note the difference in the funds-flow perspective. In the centralized budget mode, expenses flow to business from the big central revenue pool. In the RCM version, net revenues flow out of business to the university. RCM-based funds-flow analyses bring revenues to the forefront and differentiate them on the basis of the "markets" governing school-specific enrollment and research. RCM thus enables leaders and stakeholders to understand individual revenue streams and diversification among them. In turn, this leads to more sophisticated development of business cases for growth.

PORTFOLIO ANALYSIS:
COMPARISONS ACROSS UNITS

Typical RCM portfolio analysis starts with comparing fully loaded margins across schools, then moving quickly to ask why they differ. Understanding the interplay among academic quality and priority, revenue-generating capacities, and relative costs of instruction and research across competing programs is facilitated by RCM—and is absolutely vital to its effective deployment. Central systems tend to engage only in benefit analysis, while RCM makes cost-benefit calculations possible. RCM forces deans to determine their most valuable programs on both a qualitative and financial bottom line basis. If programs are low in quality and high in subsidy, the opportunity costs of protecting them are dear. Quantifying such opportunity costs enables the case for change.

A variety of productivity ratios can be developed as well when numbers of faculty, staff, and students are combined with financial data for each center. Examples such as tuition equivalent student per salary equivalent faculty, sponsored research dollars per salary equivalent faculty, and subvention per total revenue by center and across time can be particularly illuminating. Needless to say, these ratios should not be identical across centers. Different teaching methodologies, lifestyles, laboratory needs, revenue opportunities, and histories all contribute to different measures. But these measures should be consistent with quality perceptions or expectations, with institutional priorities, and with understandings of relative costs of educational methodologies. If they are not, explicit actions should be taken to realign these measures over time.

MARGIN ANALYSIS:
THE FULL COSTS OF GROWTH (OR DECLINE)

Higher education tends to calculate only the marginal direct costs and attendant revenues of expansion, shrinkage, or new initiatives. Most at-the-margin revenue-sharing deals between deans and provosts in centralized budgeting universities are designed this way, and when the deals expand, unanticipated problems arise. Cumulative effects on service units can be severe, yet go unattended.

By allocating indirect costs to centers, RCM is a standing reminder that direct expense and revenue growth can increase related indirect costs—either because new space or administrative service levels are required or because one center's growth relative to other centers may attract a larger share of allocated costs. In RCM, margin analysis includes *all* revenues and costs (additional space requirements, for example) and should include neighborhood effects (for example, the impact on arts and sciences of planned growth in engineering majors).

Consider academic partnerships with outside providers. These are typically revenue-sharing agreements between a department or school and a third-party partner who may provide international student recruitment, online learning programs, forms of executive or certificate education, and the like. In some of these agreements, the third-party partner retains 60% to 80% of revenues. Deans often like these deals because they appear to provide valuable discretionary revenues. Unplanned and unforeseen indirect costs, however, can creep up to consume the anticipated positive margin. All too frequently, the deans retain their 40% to 20% margins even as central administration incurs more costs. The typical marginal analysis that includes only direct costs would not reveal that.

SERVICE COST ANALYSIS

Determining the reasonableness of administrative and service unit costs, and their recoveries through the indirect cost recovery (F&A) rate, starts with two primary questions:

How are we prioritizing administrative or service cost? This question points to the relative levels of expenses across cost pools. Looking at our illustrative university in Table 3, we see on line 28 in the far right Total column $30 million spent on indirect academic support and on line 32, $19.5 million on research administration. Are these reasonable relative to total direct instruction and research and expenses? By what measures or benchmarks? With respect to research how does the effective indirect cost recovery (F&A) compare with what the negotiated rate would produce? Do these differ across schools—that is, are some schools involuntarily cost sharing more than others? The difference between effective and negotiated recovery rates is a measure of the subsidy of research from other revenue resources.

What is my share of the administrative or service cost, and what am I getting for it? Knowing what a given service costs them, deans can ask whether the costs are too high for the services experienced and whether they can do better on their own, either internally or through outsourcing. Facilitating conversations about service costs can keep administrative centers honest and help satisfy deans—especially when answers are grounded in good performance benchmarks. In the best of worlds, such interactions, facilitated by senior management, lead to service-level agreements between central administration units and those who pay for them.

Charging for administrative costs explicitly enables users to compare costs from alternative providers. Even when institutional considerations require that the services be provided internally, this comparison is a powerful motivator to provide more efficient services. And the explicit allocation of certain services, such as space-related costs, printing, and computing, can actually change usage patterns in the centers.

SUBVENTION/INDIRECT REVENUE ANALYSIS

All budgeting explicitly or implicitly expresses and quantifies the next years of the enterprise's plan. Unfortunately, many organizations' plans contain little more than lofty phrases lifted from a mission statement, and their annual budgets are often simple econometric projections of their prior-year budgets, sometimes not even reconciled to actual performance.

But good, bad, or indifferent, these budgets express and quantify plans. The important distinction of RCM is its explicit requirement to express relative priorities for different institutional activities through the portion of the subvention not devoted to unit price/cost imbalances. This requirement cannot be relegated to econometric projection. Because subvention is so public and so obviously indicates relative priority, it focuses attention both on the centers vying for relative favor and on the institutional leadership dispensing the favor. But recall that some differences in subvention or indirect revenue levels are the result of intentional redistributions to offset differing costs of instructions attended by uniform tuition pricing. Explicit "side letters" are needed to explain the composition of simple numbers.

Other important analyses are not directly facilitated by RCM. For example, RCM does not inherently lend itself to balance sheet analysis—unless the institution uses an all-funds approach (See Tables 2 and 3 in Chapter 3). Calculations such as return on investment and return on assets are not typically tied to RCM because most models focus on income and expense statements and not balance sheets.

RCM models do, however, have inherent linkages. Responsibility centers' bottom-line actuals contribute to increases (or decreases) in current-fund balances and, over time, can raise the question of the appropriate sizes of accumulated balances for each center. In addition, RCM models naturally link to the capital budget because each center is responsible for the debt service required of its new facilities. Therefore, the forecasting of operating and capital budgets—especially the latter's debt-financing component—need to go hand in hand.

A CLOSER LOOK AT COMPARATIVE ANALYSIS

The wealth of financial data intrinsic to an RCM model facilitates a number of comparative analyses at both the university and the school/college level. It can be useful, for example, to employ RCM data to develop comparative performance ratios such as tuition equivalent students per salary equivalent faculty, or salary equivalent faculty per dollar of research revenue or gift revenue. The following example presents an analysis of faculty productivity using sample data from Texas Tech University for FY2010.

This ASIF example—*as if* the university employed an RCM model—does not focus on individual faculty. Rather, it builds on the collegial nature of faculty work within colleges by developing measures for comparative financial performance of groups of faculty at the college and university level. The financial productivity data considered by TTU were normalized using a metric called "salary equivalent faculty" (SEF), which was calculated as a college's total faculty salary expenses (including adjuncts) divided by the college's average tenure track faculty salary. This allowed comparison across colleges of different sizes, permanent versus part-time faculty practices, and missions.

The State of Texas distributes the formula funding in the state appropriation to the different Texas universities via weighted student credit hours (WSCH), weighted by the average cost of instruction for different disciplines across all Texas public institutions. TTU employs the same WSCH to distribute tuition revenue to its individual colleges. This practice compensates, in part, for inherent differences in the unit costs of instruction between the different disciplines. Over time, variation has developed in the relative revenues and expenses across the colleges. Some of that variation is intentional, done to account for perceived relative contributions of the different disciplines and colleges to the overall university mission. But some of the variation is probably due to the different negotiating skills of the college deans and faculties.

TTU presented the financial productivity data in three categories—unrestricted revenue, unrestricted expense, and other revenue—for all colleges together and the high and low range among the individual colleges. Excerpts from the first two categories follow.

Unrestricted Revenue Comparisons

Tuition Revenue per SEF. For all TTU colleges, the average tenure track faculty member, with a salary of $84,124, benefits of $21,595, and total compensation of $105,719, produced $167,831 in revenue from tuition. This measure reflects both the teaching intensity and the WSCH of the different colleges. It ranges from a high of $242,914 in law to a low of $92,996 in visual & performing arts.

Unrestricted Direct Revenue per SEF. Direct revenue includes tuition, fees, and all other unrestricted revenues. The average tenure track faculty member with a salary of $84,124, benefits of $21,595, and total compensation of $105,719, produced $201,957 in revenue from all direct unrestricted sources (which includes the $167,831 from tuition).

Unrestricted Indirect Revenue per SEF. In the TTU model, indirect revenue is funded by certain elements of the state appropriation, student fees, and other unspecified general revenue. The provost and president award this indirect revenue to the colleges to account for different unit costs and fund new priorities. For example, the net total indirect revenue in FY2010 was $68,300,684, and the average indirect revenue per tenure track faculty member was $61,201. This differential subsidy per SEF ranged from a high of $154,345 in law to a low of $16,175 in arts and sciences.

Unrestricted Total Revenue per SEF: Total revenue includes both direct and indirect revenue. Thus, all colleges earned $263,158 in revenue from all unrestricted sources for each SEF, with an average salary of $84,124, benefits of $21,595, and total compensation of $105,719. This measure ranges from a high of $419,055 in law to a low of $165,091 in education.

Unrestricted Expense Comparisons

Unrestricted Direct Expense per SEF. On average, in FY2010, it cost the TTU colleges $175,403 per faculty member in direct operating expenses, including the total average faculty compensation of $105,719. This measure ranges from a high of $302,980 in law to a low of $116,767 in education.

Unrestricted Indirect Costs per SEF: Indirect costs are charged to the TTU colleges for services provided by the administrative service centers. Expenses are from the offices of the president, provost, chief financial officer, and vice president of research and include space-related costs for utilities, custodial, and maintenance in the space occupied by the colleges and administration. The average college incurs $87,755 in indirect costs per SEF, and these overhead costs range from a high of $134,248 in engineering to a low of $48,324 in education. One obvious reason for the higher relative administrative costs in engineering is the space intensity of engineering education and research, but another is the need for administrative (and space-related) services to support the higher relative activity (largely research in engineering) supported by restricted funds.

Unrestricted Total Expense per SEF. Total expense includes both direct and indirect costs. For the average TTU college in FY2010, this measure was $263,158. Because the indirect revenues were set to balance total unrestricted revenue and total unrestricted expense in the model, this measure is equal to unrestricted total revenue per SEF.

In full operation of RCM, the indirect revenue for individual colleges and other centers would be set in advance by the president and provost, with the expectation that the centers would budget and earn sufficient additional direct revenue to cover their total expenses (indirect as well as direct). Year-end surpluses would be banked for future programmatic or capital use, and year-end deficits would become an obligation for repayment from planned future year surpluses.

CHAPTER EIGHT

Getting to RCM: Recommended Implementation Steps

RCM has become sufficiently widespread to have collected baggage, both good and bad. It involves money in a new way, so some people will focus on how they can make (or get) more, while others will worry about their money being taken away. Many deans and auxiliary managers in centralized systems believe their revenues (undocumented) exceed their costs (incomplete), meaning others depend financially on them—which is easy to say in the absence of data. Facing the prospect of RCM, deans may fear the "real" numbers will undo their stories.

In addition to offering new opportunities, RCM imposes new responsibilities. Some people in leadership positions will not grasp how to take advantage of the former, while others will not embrace the latter. And not least: RCM represents the unknown. Even critics of current budgetary ways may discover latent reservoirs of affection for the devil they already know.

RCM initiatives, therefore, must acknowledge and engage an irony. As an institution seeks a solution for the whole—structured common rules, responsibilities, and processes—it must work through the natural decentralization we have pointed up in prior chapters to bring sense to the whole. Indeed, RCM implementations can appear as impositions of greater central control if not collaboratively managed. We need also to emphasize that academic governance is a major part of decentralization and must be engaged in any RCM implementation.

GENERAL GUIDELINES

Here are a dozen general guidelines to help keep RCM implementation on track:

1. **Confirm and animate executive leadership.** Senior leaders must be fully engaged. The president, provost, and chief financial officer (CFO) need to define, agree upon, and articulate the problems they want to solve with a new approach to resource management. They must be comfortable with redistributions of responsibility and authority. Leadership alignment with respect to the basics is a necessary condition for success. For example, you don't want a CFO breaking away from the leadership team after realizing his or her own control over allocation of certain resources would be diminished (which has actually happened).

2. **Identify key entrepreneurs.** Every university has some, sometimes many, entrepreneurs looking for incentives to perform. Find them, engage them, and appoint them to serve on implementation committees.

3. **Elicit pre-implementation stakeholder input.** Conduct a handful of focus groups to elicit stakeholders' concerns with—and the pathologies inherent in—the current approach to budgeting. Ask the stakeholder groups to describe the characteristics they would like to see in a new system. Their feedback will inform the initial specification of a new budgeting approach and serve as key reference points as new models take shape. This is a form of pre-implementation buy-in.

4. **Keep an academic focus front and center.** Constantly emphasize and demonstrate that RCM is a means to an academic ends. Early on, for example, create and share examples of how local ownership of revenues and the opportunity to grow them can advance academic goals more directly. Or, discuss how uniform budget performance accountability standards can positively affect the whole institution.

5. **Deploy a steering committee.** Given the complexity and implications of transforming a budget model, charge a steering committee of key stakeholders with overseeing implementation. The committee should primarily comprise individuals in key academic leadership and budget staff roles who understand and embrace the basic rationale for change and can easily communicate with fellow stakeholders. The committee should include members of the executive team, key deans, academic senators, and school and central budget staff. One might also want to invoke one of Cohen's and March's maxims for how to get things done in "organized anarchies" by facilitating some degree of opposition participation . The Goldilocks principle applies to the committee's size: not too large, not too small.

6. **Develop guiding principles.** Principles provide touchstones during development. Against these principles you can test everything from proposed allocation rules, to degrees of devolution of authority and responsibility, to the balance of subvention authority vis-à-vis devolved revenue ownership. Consensus on guiding principles facilitates consensus around design specifics. Chapter 3 contains guidelines that the University of Southern California used in its implementation and in subsequent troubleshooting exercises.

   Principles governing the transition period from the old budget to a new RCM budget are crucial here. No unit should pay an immediate price just because budget approaches change. Most universities moving to RCM invoke a *hold-harmless starting point* according to which the new RCM budgets are balanced through subvention to preserve the former "base" expense budgets. Then the system goes live as the new fiscal period unfolds.

7. **Develop broad-based involvement.** Committee members should regularly engage multiple stakeholder groups, such as the faculty senate, staff senate, and auxiliary enterprise leaders—especially the athletics director—by requesting feedback and sharing progress on the overall system design. Be sure to facilitate opposition participation (a la Cohen and March). Ensure outreach activities are frequent and visible across the institution.

   But the more participation, the greater number of special circumstances that arise. Thus explicit and intense efforts to obviate excess complexity are needed. Design and implementation initiatives are commonly stalled by statements such as, "We are unique, and the proposed changes should not apply to us." It's a natural response as deans among others attempt to preserve what they see as their current beneficial circumstances—and thus to create self-serving carve-outs. As these considerations are evaluated, and at times adopted, RCM models can become overly complex and implementation timelines can suffer.

8. **Create enthusiasm for the model's potential.** Leaders must understand and be prepared to discuss the multiple paths to institutional (academic) success enabled by an RCM model. Although RCM models use a consistent set of institutional rules, the rules are not the end game. Create enthusiasm by highlighting how such rules can unleash latent entrepreneurship, lead to revenue growth and increased investment in strategic priorities, and help develop a dynamic between school- and discipline-specific initiatives and investment in the commons. If stakeholders begin to view the rules as restrictive, they will focus on gaming the rules.

9. **Customize the model.** All RCM models devolve revenues, allocate costs, and include a mechanism for the executive team to capture resources to steer the institution. With the exception of these three central elements, every model is different. To customize RCM, establish rules that work within your operating environments and align with your institution's guiding principles. Do not attempt a wholesale adaptation of another institution's model.

10. **Keep the model simple.** Revenue and cost allocation rules can be complex, and academics will undoubtedly argue all sides of any allocation algorithm. Accept the reality that no perfect algorithm exists; stakeholders must seek a reasonable balance between simplicity and the desire for precision. To drive change and be effective, incentives imbedded in rules must be simple enough that, say, center directors can quickly estimate their net revenues as they contemplate various initiatives, including the occupation of additional space.

11. **Evaluate diligently, but implement quickly.** While haste can breed failure, the search for flawlessness brings its own perils. Numerous institutions, for example, have stalled at various stages of RCM implementation because their stakeholders are "never quite ready" to make the switch. Actively manage the balance between flawlessness and momentum, keeping in mind that a university should take no more than two years to implement RCM.

12. **Communicate, communicate, and communicate.** Silence is not golden. Anxieties grow inversely to the amount of information available: The absence of information makes the heart grow darker. When faculty and staff members are left to wonder how change will impact them, opposition can build and halt momentum. To avoid this situation, develop and commit to aggressive communication plans involving core messages. And heed this advice offered by an executive managing a complex change process in a major university: "Create the most comprehensive communication plan you can imagine—then triple it."

CORE MESSAGES

Communication about the RCM process, no matter what the stage of implementation, should never stop. Here are the key messages to continually share with faculty, staff, and other stakeholders:

- The university's current approach to resource management is not sustainable because: 1)..., 2)..., 3).... This is the best response to the inevitable questions "Why are we doing this?" and "What problems are we trying to solve?"

- The proposed RCM model comports with broadly accepted guiding principles. (List the principles again.)

- The model enables and rewards entrepreneurship through shared revenue ownership.

- The proposed RCM model enables cost/benefit tradeoffs by connecting revenues and their associated expenses. This means we can better direct resources to strategies that provide high academic return relative to their net costs.

- Deans need greater responsibility and authority to work with faculty members directly to manage their colleges strategically. Being closer to the action, they are often the best qualified to understand their student and research "markets" and to make academic-related financial decisions.

- Budgeting is not a zero-sum game. The objective is to use a uniformly accessible set of incentives to enable a positive-sum game.

- RCM does not introduce new expenses, but it does create the opportunity to examine allocated costs with respect to the quality of service delivered.

- RCM does not suggest that all university activities should be "profitable." Quality considerations and strategic priorities may well warrant inter-divisional transfers.

- Subvention funds will accrue to schools and colleges to support university-wide academic priorities. These priorities, and how they affect allocations, will be made explicit.

- RCM implementation is a multi-year process, and some decisions take time. We are committed to periodically reviewing and refining the approach as warranted. (This message helps calm concerns about "What's going to happen in later years?")

THE ADVANTAGES OF CRISES AND INTERNAL PRESSURES

Timing and the times matter. Current times, when key sources of revenues like state appropriations and endowment distributions have been dropping severely, provide strong impetus to develop new sources of revenues and hence to create distributed incentives to do so. Several universities are using the crisis to motivate change and positively taking advantage of the times.

Other universities have used internal bickering and back-biting about the pile up of deals apparently advantaging some schools at the expense of others as the foundation on which to launch a rationalization of the overall incentive structure. This approach is using the times to advantage. For more on this, see Curry in Massy (1976).

A FIVE-PHASE APPROACH

Organizational complexity and change management capacity vary across institutions, so RCM implementation approaches and timeframes will vary as well. Some institutions adopt RCM in as little as 18 months, while others struggle with implementation for as long as five years. Whatever the timeframe, a phased approach works best. The activities and milestones of each of the five phases are described below.

Phase I: Due Diligence and Visioning

To initiate this phase, steering committee members interview stakeholders through facilitated focus groups. The goals are to identify the financial issues facing the university—the external market, as it were—assess the strengths and weaknesses of the current budget model, and compare opportunities inherent in alternate approaches to budgeting. Ideally, group discussions should focus on these four elements:

1. **Market overview.** Participants and facilitators discuss the institution's strengths and weaknesses in multiple markets, such as students, research, philanthropic, and state support.

2. **Resource allocation approaches.** After reviewing alternative resource allocation approaches, participants have a broader context for discussing the strengths and weaknesses of the institution's current approach. It is helpful to have available a *current funds-flow model* for the most recent fiscal year, showing all sources and uses of funds and documenting the rules governing allocations. This will set the stage for comparison with other approaches.

3. **Desired characteristics and applicable principles.** Participants put forward what they would like to see in a new approach. They may mention characteristics such as transparency, data accuracy, clear accountability structure, revenues matched with expense, operating budgets connected to balance sheets, and rules enabling entrepreneurship. Guiding principles may emerge from these focus groups as well. Stakeholders will buy in to what they discover about themselves and their university far faster than they will when others impose learning on them.

4. **Budget redesign.** The facilitated analysis and discussions that occur in the focus groups ground the case for change and lead to preliminary design sketches of a new budgeting system. At this point, steering committee members might select key elements of RCM alternatives and begin framing a customized budgeting model.

This phase concludes with a report, drafted by the steering committee, that documents the case for change and the desired direction—in this case, toward a version of RCM.

Phase II: Financial Modeling

The second phase focuses on the build-out of a pro forma budget model—an ASIF model, showing the budget as if the institution already had an RCM system in place. Multiple stakeholders need to be engaged in this simulation and testing phase so they can answer these questions for themselves: What will my college or school look like in the new model? What is my college going to do?

Base the model on the most recently closed fiscal year to reduce dissonance with actual expenses and revenues. This phase demands material data: general ledger data, alignment of the chart of accounts with the proposed accountability structure, and selected unit-specific operational data such as student and employee headcounts, credit hours taught, numbers of majors, square footage occupied and costs per square foot. Using preliminary allocation assumptions, the model should portray college-level operating performance.

This base model becomes the platform for testing various alternatives and scenarios. Scenarios will evoke questions about the legitimacy of bottom-line revelations and prompt discussion of better alternatives. They will also encourage questions about charging the same tuition for programs with different costs of delivery and prompt challenges to the legitimacy of current budgets. The continued give-and-take should yield enlightenment and convergence on a single model.

Model optimization seeks the right balance between simplicity of rules and accuracy of financial portrayal; between local and central ownership of revenues; and, in general, consistency with desired characteristics and guiding principles. Document this entire effort.

As noted in the case studies in Chapter 5, several universities have redesigned their RCM structures in search of more central leverage to address new issues, including hard economic times. This suggests that, as the preferred model comes into focus, the institution should simulate a variety of potential financial stresses and assess what actions would be taken—and by whom—and whether those responses are feasible under extreme conditions. Such tests could prompt redesign of the structure—changing the size and robustness of the subvention pool, for example.

Phase III: Consensus Building

As central administrators, deans, administrative service units, and auxiliaries see themselves in new budget guises, they'll reinterpret themselves accordingly and simulate how they would manage the incentives built into the structure. Various degrees of ownership develop in this phase; it's the role of the steering committee to coalesce the work into a preferred model that reflects internal consensus.

Like the first phase, this one focuses on communication, constituency involvement, and broad consensus building—this time with a greater sense of reality than before. The communication-feedback-react cycle that occurs in this phase further refines the model.

Phase IV: Infrastructure Development

The fourth phase of implementation concentrates on the infrastructure necessary to support the RCM model. RCM requires robust, timely, and unit-specific reporting and forecasting capability, with the model populated directly from the enterprise financial system—the book of record—and data bases supporting revenue and cost allocations.

This phase also focuses on the central administrative and service units' abilities to address questions about the quality of services they provide per dollar. The conversion from internal monopolies to service-intense, cost-effective providers does not happen easily. In particular, service units will need to benchmark and justify their costs against peers and potential outsourcers; otherwise, the centers paying the indirect costs will likely demand reductions.

Phase V: Managing the System

In addition to key central players steering the process, the university may appoint a budget advisory committee. This committee brings together key stakeholders to review and critique contemplated academic initiatives, proposed tradeoffs among key planning parameters (such as tuition pricing, salary setting, and benefits changes), and the overall effectiveness of the chosen RCM model. In a real sense, this committee continues the stakeholder participation so important to the system's successful implementation.

It's also helpful to appoint a costs and services committee. This group comprises clients of central services, who review the administrative units' costs relative to the quality of services provided and make recommendations about tradeoffs.

Even after these five phases conclude, RCM management remains a continuous process. The institution will need to occasionally make real-time adaptations as critical issues arise and revisit the RCM system during scheduled periodic reviews. In other words, an *RCM System Maintenance Program* needs to be put in place. All incentives beget games, but knowing the rules creates the opportunity for compensatory and structural redesigns.

CHAPTER NINE

The Role of Financial Leadership

As we have worked our way through prior chapters addressing, "How is RCM working?" we have said a lot about what kinds of management it takes for RCM to live up to its promise. In particular, we have focused on the kind of relationship that RCM creates between provost and dean. And indeed that's what's really new in RCM. Since deans report to provosts, and RCM allocates new authority and responsibility to deans, the accountability line between them is crucial to academic and operational success. Line authority is all about accountability. So, where do CFOs fit in? Every which way!

First, CFOs are usually responsible to the president and the two together to the trustees for overall annual financial performance: the change in net assets from operations and the balance sheet—investments and capitalized physical assets. Consequently, the CFO must review the revenue and expense projections and attendant proposed budgets of the schools, challenge poorly grounded proposals, and facilitate changes as required to gain the confidence of trustees in the overall budget presented to them.

Second, the controller's office, independent of the budget office and typically reporting to the CFO, should be responsible for RCM reporting of budget vs. actual, say each month, and developing methodologies with school business officers periodically to project year end for each center. Projections are based on budget vs. actual performance to date and historical play-outs of revenue realization and expenses per month. The separation of duties here, with the controller reporting on the performance of the budget director's budget, is important. On the other hand, controller, budget director and school business officers all need to work together to understand variances from budget, to develop joint mid-year strategies to restore balance as necessary, and transfer the knowledge gained to the planning of the next year's budget.

Third, as primary keeper of the balance sheet, the CFO is responsible for university liabilities, and hence levels of and increments to debt. Deans and their business officers would work through the CFO as they develop debt-financing options for proposed capital projects, and through the provost to prioritize access to debt across the schools. *Worthy of note here is the fact that the allocation of debt access is another form of central leverage in RCM, a kind of balance-sheet subvention pool.*

Fourth, and perhaps most important overall, the CFO needs to morph from what has often been the primary role of chief accountant to strategic financial advisor not only to the president but also to the provost, deans, and auxiliary directors. While not relinquishing key control roles, CFOs should enable more than they deny.

Budget directors have major roles in RCM as well. Specifically they:

- Inform the provost and CFO/CAOs of overall financial prospects for the budget being planned, assembling key internal studies affecting enrollment, tuition and financial aid changes, competitiveness of faculty and staff salaries in their respective marketplaces, and the like.

- Develop initial planning estimates of next year's revenues and indirect cost allocations to inform deans and auxiliary directors as they develop their center budget proposals.

- Review, vet, and summarize incoming budget proposals for senior leaders.

- Work with admissions officers and school business officers to reconcile top-down projections of enrollments with school-specific estimates.

- Orchestrate budget hearings between provost and deans and between administrative directors and CFO or chief administrative officer.

- Finalize all centers budgets into a balanced whole, bringing everything together and loading the financial system for the new budget year.

- Staff and serve on the *budget steering committee* (if applicable). Typically co-chaired by the provost and CFO, the committee includes the controller, director of sponsored research, chief investment officer, and the head of enrollment management. It meets at key stages of budget development to assess progress and set parameters and prices, review performance vs. budget, address interventions as needed, finalize the budget for the coming year, and review draft financial statements. Such a central role is often complemented by a more distributed stakeholder committee.

- Staff and serve on a *budget advisory committee* (if applicable). Such committees are often chaired by a dean or senior and financially knowledgeable faculty member and comprise representatives from the deans' council, faculty and staff senates, student government, and individual faculty and administrative staff. They review, discuss, and opine on the major tradeoffs among salaries, benefit costs, tuition prices, aid policies, expense budget inflation, and the overall mix's relationship to university priorities.

The budget officer provides the glue that holds the whole process together.

CHAPTER TEN

In Summation

How have our conclusions from the first edition changed some 11 years later?

The persistence and current state of RCM among long-standing practitioners substantiate the early expectations for enabled entrepreneurship and key aspects of efficiency and effectiveness. With the right design and engaged leadership, RCM is living up to its promises of clarifying roles and responsibilities between local and central units, coupling academic authority with financial responsibility, linking cause and effect through revenue and indirect cost allocations, and incentivizing resource development and financial accountability.

As new testimony to whether RCM is working, we cite the sheer growth in RCM institutions since we wrote on the subject in 2002. Indeed, as the times change and the economic prospects of states diminish, we are not surprised at the growth. In many ways, the Great Recession is reprising the terrible economy of the 70s and early 80s, a period we have characterized as the "Great Inflation" with its adverse impacts on investments, employment, and state revenues. The response among many universities to the recent and continuing economic malaise has been much the same as before: to unleash more hunter gatherers and to seek greater operating efficiencies. The increasing rate of adaptation is essentially a market test of the value of RCM!

We also note the generally positive conclusions we found during our literature review. Indeed, even after identifying downsides of RCM, most writers acknowledged that an appropriately regulated RCM system represented an improvement over centralized budget and financial management. The staying power and ability to intelligently adapt to changing worlds of early adopters like Penn, Indiana, and Michigan further affirm our earlier positive conclusions. And reversions to old ways or outright abandonment among RCM institutions as best we have documented are minimal.

But the old criticisms and new lessons learned make very clear that formal decentralized management requires never-ending vigilance to assure that the fundamental incentives are not being subverted, and a major commitment from institutional leaders to work within and appropriately adapt the system. RCM works best with strong deans and strong provosts, CFOs, and presidents. Dynamic engagement and constructive tension are necessary to match the will of the parts with the way of the whole. We made a similar point in 2002. And we make it even more emphatically again as the most compact expression of what we have learned in the last 11 years.

BIBLIOGRAPHY

Biedenbach, Dave and Darin Wohlgemuth. Integrated Planning in a Decentralized Organization. National Association of College and University Business Officers. Annual Meeting. July 31 2012.

Bichsel, Jacqueline. Analytics in Higher Education, EDUCAUSE Center for Applied Research, 2012.

Burke, Joseph C. Fixing the Fragmented University: Decentralization with Direction. Wiley, 2007.

Cantor, N. E., & Courant, P. N. (1997, November 26). Budgets and budgeting at the University of Michigan—A work in progress. Ann Arbor, MI: The University Record. <http://www.umich.edu/%7Eurecord/9798/Nov26_97/budget.htm>

Cogan, Robert. "The Design of Budgeting Processes for State-Funded Higher Education Organization." The Journal of Higher Education 51 (1980): 556-565.

Cohen, Michael D. and James G. March. Leadership and Ambiguity: The American College President. Harvard Business Press, 1986

Cook, Rupert, and John Dunworth. "Budgetary Devolution as an Aid to University Efficiency." Higher Education 5 (1976): 153-167. JSTOR. 26 June 2007.

Courant, Paul N., and Marilyn Knepp, Phillip Hanlon, and Glenna L. Schweitzer. Budgeting with the UB Model at The University of Michigan. University of Michigan Office of the Provost. May 2008.

Curry, John R., Chapter 7 in Resource Allocation in Higher Education, Ann Arbor: The University of Michigan Press, 1996.

Curry, John R. "The Organizational Challenge IT and Revolution in Higher Education." Educause Review (2002): 40-48.

Curry, John R. Facilitation notes from MUSC Budgeting Conference. August 4, 2010.

Curry, John R., and Jon C. Strauss. Responsibility Centered Management: Lessons From 25 Years of Decentralized Management. Washington, D.C.: NACUBO, 2002.

Curry, J.R., "Budgeting," College and University Business Administration, Sixth Edition, Washington, D.C. : National Association of College and University Business Officers, 2000.

Chabotar, K., "Managing Participative Budgeting in Higher Education," Change, Vol. 27, No. S, (September/October 1995).

Deaton, Russ. US State Higher Education Finance Policy: History and Innovation. Tennessee Higher Education Commission. June 2011.

Diminnie, Carol B., and N. K. Kwak. "A Hierarchical Goal-Programming Approach to Reverse Resource Allocation in Institutions of Higher Learning." The Journal of the Operational Research Society 37 (1986): 59-66.

Ferreri, Linda B., and Scott S. Cowen. "The University Budget Process: a Case Study." Nonprofit Management and Leadership 3 (1993): 299-311.

Gjerding, Allen N., Celeste P. M. Wilderom, Shona P. B. Cameron, Adam Taylor, and Klaus-Joachim Scheunert. "Twenty Practices of an Entrepreneurial University." Higher Education Management and Policy 18 (2006): 83-110.

Goldstein, Larry. A Guide to College and University Budgeting, Foundations for Institutional Effectiveness. 4th Edition. National Association of College and University Business Officers. 2012.

Green, Kenneth C., Scott Jaschik, and Doug Lederman. The 2011 Inside Higher Ed Survey of College and University Business Officers. Inside Higher Ed, 2011.

Gros Louis, K. R. R., & Thompson, M. (2002). Responsibility center budgeting and management at Indiana University. In D. M. Priest, W. E. Becker, D. Hossler, & E. P. St. John (Eds.), Incentive-based budgeting systems in public universities (pp. 93–107). Northampton, MA: Edward Elgar.

Haeuser, Patricia N. "Budget and Planning." New Directions for Higher Education 111 (2000): 75-83.

Hanover Research Council. Responsibility Center Mangaement at Major Public Universities. Prepared for the University of California, Berkeley. 2008.

Hearn, James. Diversifying Campus Revenue Streams: Opportunities and Risks. American Council on Education Center for Policy Analysis. Washington, D.C., 2003. 22 June 2007.

Hearn, James, Darrell Lewis, Lincoln Kallsen, Janet Holdsworth, and Lisa Jones. "Incentives for Managed Growth: a Case Study of Incentives-Based Planning and Budgeting in a Large Public Research University." The Journal of Higher Education 77 (2007). 22 June 2007. <http://muse.jhu.edu>.

Hopkins, D. and Massey, W. Planning Models for Colleges and Universities. Stanford University Press, 1981.

Kallsen, L. A., Oju, E. C., Baylor, L. M., & Bruininks, R. H. (2001, June). An RCM Success Story? Empirical Results of Responsibility Centered Management Principles. Paper presented at the annual meeting of the Association for Institutional Research, Long Beach, CA.

Keohane, N.O., "Becoming Nimble, Overcoming Inertia," Harvard Magazine, (January-February 2001).

Kohrs, Ken, and Staney Degraff. General Fund Budget Review: a Study of Perceptions. The University of Michigan. University of Michigan Office of the Provost, 2005.

Kotter, John P. Leading Change. Harvard Business School P, 1996.

Krendrl, Kathy. EVP-PRO Report for Faculty Senate. Ohio University. Ohio University, 2007. <http://www.ohio.edu/provost/upload/EVP_PRO_Report.pdf>.

Lang, D. W. (2001). A primer on responsibility center budgeting and responsibility center management. In J. L. Yeager, G. M. Nelson, E. A. Potter, J. C. Weidman, & T. G. Zullo (Eds.), ASHE reader on finance in higher education (2nd ed., pp. 568-590).

Lingenfelter, Paul E. President, State Higher Education Executive Officers. State Higher Education Finance 2010. http://www.sheeo.org/pubs/pubs_results.asp?issueID=20

Leslie, Larry L. "Motivating Individuals: Incentives, Staff Reactions, and Institutional Effects." Higher Education Management and Policy 15 (2003): 69-88. EBSCO. 25 June 2007.

Maddox, David. "Iowa State University Resource Management Model Implementation. Stakeholder Analysis and Risk Assessment. BearingPoint, Inc. McLean, VA. August 15, 2007.

Massy, William F. Resource Allocation in Higher Education. University of Michigan P, 1996.

Massy, William F. "Using the Budget to Fight Fragmentation and Improve Quality." Fixing the Fragmented University: Decentralization with Direction. Comp. Joseph C. Burke. Anchor Co., 2006.

Milter, Richard G. "Resource Allocation Models and the Budgeting Process." New Directions for Institutional Research 49 (1986): 75-91.

Mortimer, Kenneth P. "Budgeting Strategies Under Conditions of Decline." New Directions for Institutional Research 43 (1984): 67-86.

Nelson, Keith R., and Jerry L. Scoby. Implementing Decentralized Responsibility-Centered Management with Budget Restructuring and Cutting Edge Technologies. CAUSE98, 8 Dec. 1998, EDUCAUSE. 20 June 2007 <http://www.educause.edu/ir/library/html/cnc9858/cnc9858.html>.

O'Neil Jr., H.F, E.M. Benisom, M.A. Diamond, and M.R. Moore, "Designing and Implementing an Academic Scorecard," Change, Vol. 31, No.6, (November/ December 1999).

Priest, Douglas M., William E. Becker, Don Hossler, and Edward P. St. John. Incentive-Based Budgeting Systems in Public Universities. Cheltenham, UK: Edward Elgar Limited, 2002.

Ruesink, Al, and Maynard Thompson, et. al. Report of the RCM Review Committee. Indiana University Bloomington. Bloomington: Indiana University, 1996. <http://www.indiana.edu/~obap/doc/1996_RCM_Review_Report.pdf>.

Salamon, L.B. and J .C. Strauss, "Using Financial Incentives in Academic Planning and Management," NACUBO Business Officer, (November 1979).

Santos, Jose. "Resource Allocation in Public Research Universities." The Review of Higher Education 30 (2007): 125-144.

Schick, Allen G. "University Budgeting: Administrative Perspective, Budget Structure, and Budget Process." The Academy of Management Review, 10 (1985): 794-802.

Strauss, J.C., R. Porter, and R. Zemsky, "Modeling and Planning at the University of Pennsylvania," Financial Planning Models, EDUCOM, (1979).

Strauss, J.C., "Indirect Cost Rate Reduction Through Management Action," NACUBO Business Officer, (November 1985).

Strauss, J., Curry, J., & Whalen, E. (1996). Revenue responsibility budgeting. In W. F. Massy (Ed.) (1996).

Tierney, Michael L. "Priority Setting and Resource Allocation." New Directions for Institutional Research 31 (1981): 29-43.

Theobald, Neil, and Maynard Thompson, et. al. Responsibility Centered Management at Indiana University Bloomington. Indiana University Bloomington. Bloomington: Indiana University, 2000. <http://www. indiana.edu/~obap/doc/2000_RCM_Review_Report.pdf>.

Theobald, Neil. RCM Review Assessments and Chancellor's Fund. January 2005. <http://www.indiana.edu/~vpcfo/RCM/index.shtml>.

Theobald, Neil. Responsibility-Centered Management at Indiana University Bloomington Report of the RCM Review Committee. December, 2011.

Theobald, Neil. Senior Vice President and Chief Financial Officer Department Website. Indiana University. 2012. http://www.indiana.edu/~vpcfo/RCM/index.shtml

Thomas, Harold. "Power in the Resource Allocation Process: the Impact of Rational Systems." Journal of Higher Education Policy and Management 22 (2000): 127-137. EBSCO. 26 June 2007.

Toutkoushian, R. K., & Danielsen, C. (2002). Using performance indicators decentralized budgeting systems and institutional performance. In D. Becker, D. Hossler, & E. P. St. John (Eds.), Incentive-based budgeting public universities (pp. 205–226). Northampton, MA: Edward Elgar.

Tracy, Tim. Chair of Financial Systems Accountability Committee. Committee Report. University of Kentucky. May 22, 2012.

Varghese, N. V. "Incentives and Institutional Changes in Higher Education." Higher Education Management and Policy 16 (2004): 27-39. EBSCO. 25 June 2007.

Volk, C. S., Slaughter, S., & Thomas, S. L. (2001). Models of institutional resource allocation: Mission, market, and gender. Journal of Higher Education, 72, 387–413.

Vonasek, Joseph. Implementing Responsibility Center Budgeting. Journal of Higher Education Policy and Management. September 14, 2011.

West, J. A., Seidita, V., DiMattia, J., & Whalen, E. L. (1997). RCM as catalyst: Study examines use of responsibility center management on campus. NACUBO Business Officer, August, 24–28.

Whalen, E. L. (1991). Responsibility center budgeting: An approach to decentralized management for institutions of higher education. Bloomington, IN: Indiana University Press.

Whalen, E. L. (2002). The case, if any, for responsibility center budgeting. In D. M. Priest, W. E. Becker, D. Hossler, & E. P. St. John (Eds.), Incentive-based budgeting systems in public universities (pp. 111–135). Northampton, MA: Edward Elgar.

Wilms, W. W., Teruya, C., & Walpole, M. (1997, September/October). Fiscal reform at UCLA: The clash of accountability and academic freedom. Change, 29, 41–49.

Wolfe, A., "The Feudal Culture of the Postmodern University," The Wilson Quarterly, Vol. XX, No.1 (Winter 1996).

Zemsky, R., Porter, R., & Oedel, L. P. (1978). Decentralized planning: To share responsibility. Educational Record, 59, 229–253.

Zemsky, R., Editor, "Call to Meeting," Policy Perspectives, Vol. 4, No. 4 (February 1993).

Zemsky, R. and W.E. Massy, "Expanding Perimeters, Melting Cores, and Sticky Functions: Toward an Understanding of Current Predicaments," Change, Vol. 27, No.6 (November/December 1995).

Zeppos, Nicholas S. (2010, May/June). Centralizing a university's financial decision making. Trusteeship magazine, 14-19.

APPENDIX A

Illustrative List of Institutions with RCM and RCM-Like Models

American University

Case Western Reserve

Central Michigan University

Cleveland State University

Claremont Graduate University

Cornell University

Duke University

Dominican University of California

Emory University

Florida International University

Harvard University

Indiana University

Indiana University–Purdue University Indianapolis

Iowa State University

Kent State University

Medical University of South Carolina

northeastern university

Ohio State University

rensselaer polytechnic institute

Syracuse University

Texas Tech University

University of Alabama, Birmingham

University of Arizona

University of Cincinnati

University of Delaware

University of Denver

University of Florida

University of Idaho

University of Illinois – Urbana-Champaign

University of Michigan

University of Minnesota

University of Missouri – Kansas City

University of New Hampshire

University of Oregon

University of Pennsylvania

University of Pittsburgh

University of Rochester

University of Southern California

University of Virginia

University of Washington

Vanderbilt University

Washington University of St. Louis

Wright State University

APPENDIX B

Frequently Asked Questions

Below is a list of common RCM questions that we have fielded in recent years. Many of them arise from the model's promise verses the model's performance. In previous chapters we have addressed many of the questions proposed herein, though by way of summary for easy review.

At what sort of institution will RCM work best?

This far into the text it is clear that there have been notable successes with RCM across the institutional spectrum—private and public, large and small, unionized and nonunionized. We have found that size and complexity are the primary necessary conditions. With the obvious complexity attending combinations of arts and sciences colleges and multiple professional schools, and countless unstructured entrepreneurial activities all around, deans and faculty are more likely to understand the need for policies and procedures to bring order to—indeed to simplify—the "organized anarchy" (to use Cohen's and March's description of universities). The authors have had some experience in trying to introduce the "competitiveness" and "game playing" inherent in RCM into small college environments and found that faculty and staff are so comfortable with the notion that everything could essentially be a personal negotiation with the president that they are unwilling to subject themselves to what they perceive as RCM's straightjacket. This could account for the lack of enthusiasm encountered at Worcester Polytechnic Institute in its experiments with RCM as described earlier, but that experience could also have been influenced by the homogeneity of engineers and engineering departments as suggested later in this chapter. Our primary point: size and complexity matter.

What has been the primary reason for pullback from pure RCM?

A number of examples have been cited where administrations succeeding in the initial RCM implementation have chosen to relax some of the RCM principles noted in Chapter 2. And, as indicated in the TTU case study in Chapter 5, the founding RCM administration pulled back on the implementation at the last minute before going live. If we had to cite a single reason for this backsliding, it would come down to leadership/ management style. It turns out that it is extremely challenging to lead/ manage in the transparent environment imposed by RCM. One of RCM's great virtues is that there are no secrets. Well, it turns out that many of even our most respected and effective leaders are not comfortable with being totally open, with having to justify every decision publicly, and with not being able to enter into confidential arrangements with deans and others as part of their approach to leadership/management. Others, as many examples described here confirm, find that the RCM environment actually improves their effectiveness. It will behoove presidents and provosts and the trustees to whom they report to assess their comfort levels with these aspects of RCM before finding out the hard way that RCM won't work for them.

Other reasons for pullback have involved subversions of the accountability structure and rigidity of original design. We have noted before that in the 1980s, the University of Miami during its first year of RCM forgave deficits in some schools in such measure as to deny access to surpluses among others. The integrity of the system was compromised; the faith was broken. Very recently, initial design problems limiting the subvention pool to state appropriations (rather than, say, using a participation tax across a diversified pool of revenues) at the University of South Carolina left insufficient rebalancing resources in the hands of the provost when state appropriations declined precipitously. Revenue ownership was recentralized ("un-devolved").

Does RCM express and quantify the strategic plan?

Yes, but, as described in Chapter 8, too often only implicitly. The important distinction of RCM is the explicit requirement to express a relative priority for different institutional activities through that portion of the subvention not devoted to unit price/cost imbalances. But the numbers do not necessarily speak for themselves: Words need to grace them. We have already discussed this at length.

How do you maintain the integrity of academic programs and course offerings?

The focus on revenue growth and entrepreneurship make RCM models inherently market driven, and most markets ultimately reward quality. There are times, however, when leadership must intervene. In our 2002 book, we noted that strategic regulation should modulate laissez faire operations. Almost all universities have committees to evaluate program and course offerings, even those not employing RCM models. This type of committee should be used to ensure the integrity of academic offerings.   Among the potential alleged threats are the creation of trade barriers that impede students' abilities to take courses outside of their home departments, the development of non-core course offerings within colleges, and the easing of grading standards to arouse course demand. By employing a faculty curriculum committee, these potential risks can be somewhat mitigated, though at the end of the day, RCM is in no way leadership proof. It is the case, however, that for all the much trumpeted risk, the authors have seen very few documented cases where deans and faculty compromised academic integrity in favor of dollars.

Does RCM provide explicit recognition and support for institutional priorities?

Yes, it does—if provosts and presidents are explicit in their communications. Once there is an understanding of what portion of subvention allocations is needed to offset disparities between the appropriate costs of programs and tuition pricing, the rest is what's available to support university priorities. A standard communication attending any good budget process is the provost's statement of priorities for funding (whatever the system) at the beginning, and his or her wrap-up letter describing what was funded and why. A number of presidents and provosts, however, have found the discipline of having to make and defend relative priority decisions in public to be excessively demanding. This issue alone has accounted for the failure of several institutions to realize the full potential of RCM. A note from our case study of Penn in Chapter 5 may be apropos: The "ossification of subventions" over a period of years extinguished whatever signals relative subventions might have provided at one time.

Does RCM help realize the objectives of collegial governance?

Yes, but only if deans and department chairs avoid Alan Wolfe's negative characterization of faculty governance in Chapter 1 and involve their faculty!

RCM establishes a decision framework with its structure and underlying information on resource deployment and return. Properly involved at the local levels, faculty members can have substantive impact on resource generation, subject to normal market constraint, and on allocations of new resources as informed by their own knowledge close to the action. Faculty can now move from their all-too-frequent position of dismissible criticism to that of meaningful participation with real data and real responsibility for both success and failure.

At Penn, for example, faculty went from general criticism of what they characterized as exploitative indirect cost recovery (F&A) charges on their sponsored research grants to genuine understanding of the need to generate revenue to cover the overhead costs associated with the research program. This is not to imply, however, that they wouldn't have liked those charges to be lower. With the understanding of the real indirect costs attending research and instruction, faculty actually led the movement for indirect cost charges on restricted gift and endowment revenues at Penn to help pay for the associated overhead costs so as to relieve the otherwise inevitable burden on tuition revenue. Further, IUB's RCM Review Committee (Theobald and Thompson, 2000) indicates, "The RCM process also makes the budget more transparent to all involved and offers an opportunity for responsiveness to the needs of students and faculty."

If deans have to negotiate subvention fund requests from the provost, how is RCM any different from incremental budgeting?

At its best, RCM is an entrepreneurship and accountability model, not an autonomy model. This means that colleges and schools should play by fair and consistent rules, but that no individual unit can act on its own against the common good. The subvention fund is designed to maintain this balance: A dean's argument for subvention requires that the individual college make its case in the context of university-wide goals and priorities. Through this use of subvention, RCM creates a decentralized system integrated by the common need for subvention.

We should not over emphasize the dependence on some level of subvention, however. Typical RCM revenue allocation rules leave a lot of room for schools to design programs and fund them on their own as long as the rules remain stable. It's the combination of central steering through subvention and local entrepreneurship that can make the whole larger than the sum of the parts. The dynamic engagement involved can establish a much different budgeting milieu than the typical political one characterizing deans lobbying for incremental funding and budgets established by a handshake.

Does RCM increase the amount of focus placed on revenues?

Yes, almost always. The early experience of the University of Pennsylvania (Strauss, Porter, and Zemsky, 1979) underscores the importance of resource development. When RCM was introduced in the early 1970s, it was envisioned that deans and department heads would respond to the financial incentives to balance expenses to revenues by employing intimate local knowledge to effect dramatic changes in expense patterns. There were, in fact, dramatic changes, but almost all were focused on using local knowledge to increase revenues, and with significant success. This probably should not have been a surprise. After all, individual faculty members operating from their disciplinary departments are one of the bastions of entrepreneurship in our society. Faculty influence enrollments, control course content, establish standards and evaluate performance, select and evaluate colleagues, and develop external philanthropic and research support. In an environment that expects responsible financial behavior, faculty members have strong incentives and lots of authority to focus on revenue generation. And with good leadership, it is relatively straightforward to align these incentives for revenue generation with the furtherance of institutional mission. Penn's growth to this day strongly suggests continuing deployment of revenue incentives inherent in RCM. See again the Penn case study in Chapter 5.

A case from USC is instructive here as well. The schools of dentistry, pharmacy, and urban and regional planning literally built themselves on the enrollment and research revenue incentives of RCM. Other schools, like music, realized that, given unit costs, their further development could not come from enrollment but had to come from gifts and endowments. This recognition led to vigorous fundraising and ultimately an endowment gift sufficient to name the school: now the Thornton School of Music. Coupling of marginal revenues with marginal costs led to appropriately different strategies among the schools. See further the USC case study in Chapter 5.

Does RCM create entrepreneurs?

Entrepreneurial systems do not necessarily create entrepreneurs. Too many years of perfecting pie division turn off the pie-expanding gene. Congenital entrepreneurs will take to the RCM incentives. But provosts may have to change their deans to match entrepreneurial capability with the system's incentives.

How does RCM aid in cost/benefit analyses and tradeoff studies?

In his book on resource allocation, Bill Massy (1996) speaks at some length about the resource allocation tradeoffs between academic programs requiring subsidy, which he refers to as intrinsic, and those which generate additional resources for reallocation elsewhere, which he refers to as instrumental. By portraying what Massy calls subsidies as net revenues, or fully costed margins (or indirect revenues), RCM leads immediately to questions of program quality and priority relative to bottom lines. We have seen examples of all kinds: programs with high academic quality generating positive net revenues, and other programs of similar quality needing subsidies; programs with low academic quality requiring subsidy, with other similar quality programs generating positive net revenues. Understanding the relative academic value and revenue-generating capacities of competing academic programs is absolutely vital to RCM's effective deployment.

See Chapter 7 for further analytic approaches and examples of their utility.

Does RCM facilitate the responsible management of entrepreneurial activities?

Yes, mostly. Zemsky and Massy (1995) explain the apparently paradoxical growth of new research institutes at the periphery of many institutions during times of seeming financial constraint. Here, the incentives for external funding have fomented the growth of faculty-centered professional and research activities as add-ons at the margin of the traditional discipline based departmental structure. In many a university today, similar activities are growing rapidly, often in relatively unstructured ways; distance learning is among the most prominent. Such growth at the periphery is not necessarily bad so long as the activities do not detract from the core institutional missions of teaching and research and that these "marginal" activities pay for their proportionate share of indirect support costs. But with RCM, such growth need not be peripheral at all. Indeed, growth can be absorbed into a standing center, and aligned with the departmental and core institutional missions to provide significant additions of talent, facilities, and resources to the milieu. Developing and responding to revenue opportunities is at the core of RCM, not at the periphery.

The experience of the University of Denver is compelling. In the late 1980s, Denver's indicators of financial health were pointing and moving in the wrong direction. A new administration diagnosed the core problem succinctly: A disconnect existed between revenue-related decisions in admission, enrollment, and program selection on the one hand, and the level of expense authority committed to in the budget on the other. University revenues were not keeping pace with expense growth, but the impacts were not immediately visited upon the schools responsible. Denver changed the rules, forcing the coupling of choice with consequences, by implementing RCM. Denver's financial (and academic) health indicators have been pointing strongly upward ever since, although Craig Woody, Denver's vice-chancellor of financial affairs, reports that several changes in deans along the way were necessary. Lines of business have to be chosen strategically and well when the chooser wins or loses from the choice.

We note, however, the proliferation of general education courses in the professional schools at USC discussed in Chapter 6; the cumulative consequences were perverse and required leaders to intervene. We reiterate *ad nauseam*: RCM enables entrepreneurs but it does not create them, and empowers managers, but does not replace them.

Should deans devolve RCM to departments within their colleges/schools?

We have noted that not all deans are compatible with RCM; the same applies to department chairs, and the sheer magnitude of department chairs amplifies this challenge. In general, we suggest that deans deploy discretionary resources within their colleges/schools, using their knowledge of revenues earned and expenses incurred in the departments, but not fully implement the RCM model down to the department level. However, recognizing that this answer is somewhat equivocal, we revert to acknowledging the importance of each institution's and its divisions' contexts.

In 2008, Hanover Research conducted an informal survey of 10 leading RCM institutions and found that among the institutions, 60% used their model to manage at the college and school level, while 40% devolved the model to department chairs.

In principle, RCM models can be effective at any level of an organization in which there is the ability to impact revenues. In fact, RCM mirrors, in many ways, the model used in the United States for funded research: individual faculty members write grant proposals, develop budgets, estimate indirect costs (based on an indirect cost recovery (F&A)rate), secure funding, and are then held accountable to deliver within budget. This suggests that the RCM model might usefully be devolved to the faculty level.

If deans do make the decision to devolve their RCM model to the department level, we do recommend additional diligence. Devolving the model to departments increases model complexity, introduces a new level of overhead allocations, requires additional explicit balancing between the haves and have-nots (perhaps requiring a sub-subvention pool), and limits the dean's flexibility to invest in larger strategic activities. Moreover, in our experience, the effectiveness of departmentally based RCM can vary significantly with disciplines because, in addition to entrepreneurship, RCM favors a competitive spirit between centers. At Penn, for example, we have noted that engineers and engineering departments are so united by their disciplinary commonalities that they had difficulty doing anything that would appear to disadvantage a fellow engineer or department. Arts and science departments on the other hand appeared to have little qualms in that regard, stemming no doubt from the enormous gulf between say physicists and sociologists. Arts and sciences faculty and departments appeared to be perfectly comfortable with benefiting at the apparent expense of their fellows because, other than their own humanity, they had so little in common. Interestingly, however, in medicine where everyone even has a common oath, there appeared to be few barriers to internal competition.

Can you make RCM perfect by continually refining the algorithms and the rules?

No! We have met and lived with academic and administrative officers who believe that perfection is only a rule change or a new rule away, and every local issue can be handled by a systemic change. These are the true believers, the fundamentalist RCM fans. Those who pursue this path are doomed to replicate 2010 federal legislation that purports to address the recent meltdown in the financial sector with 2,600 pages of legislation and hundreds of rules but does not address the core issue: too big to fail. Some rule changes do, indeed, improve structured incentives. But too many drive out entrepreneurship. Learning and complying with too many rules leaves little time for focus on academic direction: a manifestation of Gresham's law according to which bad currency drives out good currency.

We acknowledge that talk about rules is seductive stuff for smart people. But a monomaniacal focus on rules is doomed; it is ultimately all seduction and no consummation. The University of Minnesota became so consumed by debates about cost-allocation rules that its leaders had to stop and start over. Gresham at work!

The lesson: Qualitative, academic talk has to become the strong currency, by dent of leadership. Bear "keep it simple" in mind. Think 80/20. *More and ever more refined rules cannot make RCM leadership and judgment proof.*

Is RCM self-correcting when revenues decline?

Yes, more so than central budgeting systems. One of the more interesting consequences of RCM in some universities has been the broader participation of faculty and staff in the quantification and implementation of plans they help formulate. And this involvement yields more rapid adaptation to inevitable exogenous changes. This would not be possible without the direct involvement and responsibility of individuals on the front lines, so to speak, who observe the changes first—usually in their school's revenue statements—and are in the best position to respond creatively. The IUB RCM Review Committee (Theobald and Thompson, 2000) reinforces this observation, noting that "Primary among these benefits is the ability to address budgetary problems at the level closest to the action, where the information needed to respond to opportunities and cope with problems is most complete." The total quality management movement has emphasized reducing layers of hierarchical management and empowering the individual for exactly the same reason and with the same result.

A 1999 *Change* article describes how one school at USC adapted the Kaplan and Norton "balanced scorecard" approach to strengthen its case for a larger share of the provost's "academic excellence" subvention (O'Neil, Benisom, Diamond, and Moore, 1999). And IUB's RCM Review Committee (Theobald and Thompson, 2000) note: "RCM leads to greater transparencies in budgets. This has allowed the campus to better allocate its scarce resources in a time when the state appropriation plays a declining role..."

Among the most important self-corrections is that enrollment shifts are followed by commensurate tuition revenue shifts. In the 1990s and early 2000s, for instance, undergraduate enrollment shifted materially from the hard sciences to computer science across the nation. Under RCM, all else equal, the school of science would have to cut teaching costs (positions) or argue for more subvention because its revenues were down. The sciences dean would be forced, as a natural act, to recognize this problem from the school's own revenue statement. The school housing computer science, receiving its own revenue statement, would see additional revenues to hire more faculty and add course sections.

In highly centralized universities, such resource reallocations require massive central political will because provosts typically allocate faculty positions, which, once gone, become owned by the deans. Enrollment redistribution is the provost's problem to solve, since he or she owns all revenues, and the deans' agony to suffer through. Rarely in centralized systems are resources reallocated even remotely in proportion to changes in student demand. Exercise of too much political will, however, can threaten careers.

Still a different form of self-correction involves general education or distribution course requirements for undergraduates. In many state universities, students and parents in recent years have claimed that insufficient numbers of sections of required courses have delayed graduations, often up to a year or more. IU and the University of Minnesota have both reported that since the advent of RCM, this problem has diminished. Why? Because, like Willy Sutton, departments have recognized that distribution requirements are "where the money is." Crass as it may seem, the incentive led to the right outcome. But also note some of the misuses of general education courses described in Chapter 6; some aspects of RCM require intervention.

Are subventions self-correcting?

Subventions are *not* self-correcting. As Michael Masch, budget director at Penn, has pointed out, subventions can ossify. If they become entitlements through lack of frequent refreshing and renewing of their rationales, then the president and provost can lose their abilities to affect the direction of the whole. Which is to say, the whole defaults to the sum of the parts. Holding and advancing the commons requires active and aggressive leaders. See the Penn case study in Chapter 5.

It is important to also remember that subventions are not welfare. Leaders need to remember and document the parts which comprise subvention—so much for neutralizing the cost/price mismatch; so much for plan success; so much for advancing institution-wide goals; so much for promising startup ventures. If programs are academically weak, of low priority, and require subsidies, subvention can be welfare; if programs are distinguished, of high priority, and are relatively costly, their "subsidies" via subvention are strategic and smart.

Does RCM create incentives for service providers to be efficient?

This issue is typically overlooked in RCM, but as long as deans have to balance their expenses to the dual constraints of their revenues and the indirect costs "handed" to them, central services can act like monopolies and stiff their customers. Sometimes the stick is the better incentive than the carrot: Central administrative services providers need to know that they can be outsourced, and occasionally they should be, if only to make a point. Then these providers will learn that they have to know their competitors' service prices, meet or better them, or at least demonstrate greater local knowledge and better services, to earn the business of the deans. Back-pressure from the responsibility (revenue) centers appears not to be enough. Leadership needs to step up and facilitate informed decanal (and other client) pushback. The University of Denver has successfully used benchmarks and balanced scorecard assessments to control costs and improve services in conjunction with pressure from the deans. We noted in Chapter 6 that, by and large, this promise of RCM is not working well, sometimes not at all. (But even when not working well in this regard, RCM at least draws attention to the relative costs and values of administrative and space-related services, which are typically hidden in other budget approaches.)

Should provosts and chief administrative officers attempt to manage administrative services and costs in both central units and responsibility centers?

Yes. We have seen many instances of deans of centers, flush with revenues and unhappy with central services, hiring their own administrators to supplement services they are already paying for in their allocated indirect costs. In cases with a unique clientele needing focused attention, this is warranted. In other cases, it is symptomatic of an unresponsive central administration, whose failure to recognize and correct a service problem denies economies of scale and shifts costs to the deans who invoke local solutions. Engaging the issues and managing the balance are imperative. Sometimes, central service units need a budget champion to enable them to scale services to meet increased demand—even if the indirect costs allocated to and paid by the revenue-generating centers increase materially. See in particular the Penn case study in Chapter 5.

How large should institutions make subvention pools?

RCM presidents and provosts need sufficient, diverse, and liquid subvention resources. If the subvention pool begins to evaporate, or if subventions become politically hardened (i.e., become de facto entitlements), then the critical ability to steer the whole is lost. Presidents and provosts need to contribute to the growth and diversification of subvention sources by raising unrestricted gifts (for consumption or endowment) and by guarding against importunities from deans to restrict internal resources available for general use. Subvention pools need some depth as well to operate as "surge tanks." We have seen instances where precipitous drops in revenues in a center needed to be met with subventions sufficient to smooth the transition to the reduced revenue state. Narrowly diversified pools can create havoc as well. Recall our observations earlier about the University of South Carolina basically abandoning RCM when the sole source of its subvention pool, the state appropriation, decreased so quickly that the university could not reasonably protect appropriation-dependent units. *Subvention pools need to be wide and deep and never frozen.*

How do the administrative support needs of colleges change under RCM?

The support needs of colleges change in two material ways with the implementation of RCM. First and foremost, college leaders will likely need more detailed and sophisticated data with which to manage their operations. For example, once colleges are asked to forecast enrollments, they will need access to credit hour data, student enrollment data, applicant data, and retention data. In addition to these data, similar levels of detail will be needed for unit-level planning with respect to financial aid, student fees, grants and contracts, indirect cost recoveries (F&A), gifts, and sales and services. (It should be noted here, however, that very few RCM systems expect, or allow for that matter, colleges to singularly forecast undergraduate enrollments and financial aid. Most universities manage undergraduate admission and offsetting financial aid centrally, albeit in response to the needs and capacities of the individual colleges. Accordingly, the central undergraduate enrollment management unit and budget office will be in a much better position to assure that undergraduate tuition revenue and offsetting financial aid expense are forecast responsibly within individual units and in total. Similar issues pertain to other revenue and expense items that are influenced strongly by central policies and service units.)

In addition to enhanced data and reporting capabilities, colleges will need sophisticated business managers. Pat Harker, the president of the University of Delaware, explained the relative importance of this role by stating that "good business managers can deal with data issues, but even great data cannot save a mediocre business manager" (Ohio University, RCM Learning Day). The reality is that when deans are given greater financial authority and responsibility, they will need better advisors, modelers and forecasters.

Do deans need professional business officers in the schools?

Yes. In centralized budget systems, managing a direct expense budget is relatively easy. But managing a responsibility center budget requires comprehensive understanding of the center's business model: To predict and budget the center's tuition revenues, one must understand the external student recruitment market and the internal course enrollment patterns; to predict and budget indirect cost recovery (F&A) on center contracts and grants, one must know the indirect cost recovery (F&A) rate and predict the center's (modified) total direct expenses to plan and manage the annual budget; to manage total expenses, one must master the indirect cost allocation rules and the responsibility center/central service interface. Typically, smart amateurs who have grown from administrative assistants into local budget managers won't be good enough. And while they cost more, professionals will find resources for their deans that amateurs will not.

Is tension among central and local authority good for RCM institutions?

Yes. We have talked about dynamic and constructive tension in sufficiently different places to warrant singling it out as a bold bullet point. Tensions between local and central priorities are vital to dealing with the so-called *tragedy of the commons.* Tensions between the president's and provost's "industrial policy" and the deans' proclivities toward laissez faire can be more productive when explicit rather than implicit. And, tensions between the risk-taking of deans and the CFO/CAO's requirement of conservative budget balance are educational in both directions: Deans learn how financial officers think, and financial officers learn how academic leaders think.

Formally designed processes provide the vessels to engage difficult issues. Standing meetings with jointly developed agendas between central and local business officers ensure common knowledge and learning through shared expertise; similar processes keep deans, provosts, and financial officers working through dissonance toward a more common cause; and formal periodic communications around financial performance, economic and market challenges, and institutional priorities allow for broad dissemination among stakeholders.

The trick in managing RCM is to avoid the seductive tyranny of either/ or. Either we are a centrally managed economy or we are anarchical laissez faire: No, we seek the right balance. Either we are risk takers or control freaks: No, we enable some risk within reasonable, conservative bounds.

Who should manage an institution's RCM model?

RCM needs a resident intellectual champion. RCM is a structure designed to balance academic entrepreneurship with fiscal responsibility. The end game is responsible academic growth and development. RCM needs rules, which are the means to the end game.

People not raised in RCM and who inherit leadership roles in RCM universities are often captivated and captured by the rules and the legions of faculty who would change them. The rules then become the end game, and like the tax code, become ever more elaborate. Then winning is defined by litigation to effect pie redistribution. Entrepreneurship is driven out, and institutions can stagnate. Intellectual champions never lose sight of the true end game, and force academic focus and rule simplification to keep lawyers and accountants from governing the academy. At the other end of the spectrum, a well-oiled RCM system can run "open loop" for several years: With the basic inputs, deans can develop their own revenues and attendant balanced budgets and go their merry, locally optimizing ways. Recall the Penn case study in Chapter 7 wherein subventions ossified, local administration grew excessively, and most people had forgotten the intellectual foundations of the system they were using—hence Penn Vice President Bonnie Gibson's observation that the system requires an "RCM zealot." Remember also the Indiana case where education of newcomers to RCM is one of the reasons for the five-year reviews.

INDEX

ABOUT THE AUTHORS

John R. Curry is a managing director in Huron Consulting Group's higher education practice where he works with clients to develop incentive-based budgeting, assess organizational effectiveness, and create operational efficiencies. Before joining Huron in 2005, Curry served as executive vice president of the Massachusetts Institute of Technology, and prior to that was vice president for business and finance at Caltech, administrative vice chancellor and CFO at UCLA, and vice president for budget and planning at USC. The author of numerous articles on responsibility center management, implementation of enterprise software systems, and integrating budgeting with balance sheet planning, he holds a BA in physics and an MA in mathematics from West Virginia University, completed doctoral coursework in mathematics at Carnegie Mellon University, and was an NIMH fellow in organizational research at Stanford.

Andrew L. Laws is a managing director in Huron Consulting Group's higher education practice, and has worked with more than 30 institutions, helping them develop approaches for maximizing, allocating, and leveraging financial resources. He specializes in designing budget models that use incentives to drive behaviors and focus resources on institutional strategies. A frequent speaker on financial trends in higher education, he is a faculty member in Vanderbilt University's Institute for Higher Education Management. Laws received a bachelor's degree in business administration from the University of Mississippi, an MBA from the University of Chicago, and a Doctorate of Education from Vanderbilt University.

Jon C. Strauss is the president of Manhattanville College in Purchase, New York. Previously, Dr. Strauss was the interim dean of engineering at Texas Tech University. A former member of and current consultant to the National Science Board, he served as president of the Bainbridge Graduate Institute from 2008 to 2009. Strauss was the fourth president of Harvey Mudd College, serving in that position from 1997 to 2006. Prior to Harvey Mudd, he was the chief financial officer of the Howard Hughes Medical Institute. From 1985 to 1994, he served as the 13th president of Worcester Polytechnic Institute. He has also held the positions of senior vice president of the University of Southern California and vice president for budget and finance at the University of Pennsylvania. Strauss received his PhD in electrical engineering from the Carnegie Institute of Technology, his masters in physics from the University of Pittsburgh, and his bachelor's degree from the University of Wisconsin–Madison.